Carol Honour was raised in Sowerby Bridge, West Yorkshire. She was brought up in a working class family and has taken on many different working roles in her life, usually as a change driver in varying companies. She has travelled extensively to different parts of the world discovering different sights and cultures and enjoys a challenge. She was inspired to pick up a pen and start writing after invigilating an art examination at a local school.

To my mum who always made sure that I had everything I needed when I was a child, even if she had to go without.

Carol Honour

PICTURE OF DEATH

AUSTIN MACAULEY PUBLISHERS™

LONDON • CAMBRIDGE • NEW YORK • SHARJAH

A CIP catalogue record for this title is available from the British Library.

ISBN 9781398436176 (Paperback)
ISBN 9781398436183 (ePub e-book)

www.austinmacauley.com

First Published 2021
Austin Macauley Publishers Ltd®
1 Canada Square
Canary Wharf
London
E14 5AA

The unnamed gravedigger, who I met at a funeral.

The young boy was skimming pebbles, with his grandfather, laughing with joy, as they splashed over the surface of the water. The colours of the trees around them were spectacularly bright and reflected on the surface of the lake. The birds were chirping and flying in formation above them, others were hovering over the water that was sparkling like diamonds in the sunshine. His grandfather was asking him, even now, after 20 years, what do you see and feel Simon. They're watching me, gramps that's what I feel, but I can't see them…

Chapter One

Simon sat quietly in the drawing-room, as his father had instructed him. Don't forget "children should be seen and not heard" recited his mother. The long table at the end of the room was ladened with food in various shapes and colours that looked like an elaborate piece of artwork. He wasn't allowed to touch the display, let alone, eat any of it. After all, his mother explained, "It will only make you fat and your skin will look unhealthy and nobody is interested in people who do not look after their bodies." He decided that his mother probably didn't eat either, as she was thin and had flawless skin and she did appear to be very popular. The background music was something classical for 'classy' gatherings, or so he had overheard Jessy, the housekeeper, saying, laughingly, to someone on the telephone earlier.

He observed all the ladies arriving for the party, floating around, in their beautiful colourful dresses, looking like fairy princesses and wondered why all the men were dressed the same, in dark sombre colours. Standing about unobtrusively, they reminded him of the penguins that he had once seen at the zoo, where Jessy had taken him recently for his 5th birthday, as a special treat, when his parents were away.

Some of the guests had arrived, with what looked like, overnight bags, but they were so big, they could have been staying for the week, so he knew this was going to be a long night, with lots of music and fun for the grown-ups. Not that he'd be able to stay up and watch though, he thought glumly.

One or two of the women stopped to ask him how he was, but remembering his mother's words, he just replied "very well, thank you", smiled, then looked away, continuing to observe the other guests. The women came to the conclusion that they had been dismissed, which was, in this case, not a bad thing. What on earth do you say to such a young boy?

There would have had quite a different reaction if he had been in his late teens, after all, they needed to be admired, for all the effort that they had made, not to mention the cost, to look so young and stunningly beautiful. They couldn't quite understand why the boy was there in the first place but decided it was probably so that he could see them arriving in their finery. After all, they were famous people, that he more than likely, had seen on either the television or on the front cover of one of his mother's magazines.

He felt like he'd been sat there forever, although, in reality, it had only been an hour. After everyone had arrived, his father announced, whilst smiling at his guests and with his hand on Simon's shoulder, that it was, "Time for bed, young man." He stood up and politely said goodnight, and went up to his room.

Jessy had prepared him a light healthy salad supper, as instructed by his mother. He would have much preferred to have some of the food from the party's table but wasn't allowed such delights, although Jessy had sneaked him up a couple of chocolate biscuits. Grinning, he thought, *I bet mother doesn't even know that we have biscuits in the house.*

She locked his door when she left, so that no one disturbed him later during the evening, or in the early hours. These parties tended to get a bit raucous later on, with all the coming and goings and she didn't want him to become scared, if someone accidentally, tried to enter his room.

Last month, when she had been going up to her room, after clearing up, after the guests had moved upstairs, she had caught one of the men called Ron, going into Simon's room. By the time she got to the door, he was hovering over his bed, removing the bed covers and stroking the boy's head. Simon was just laying there, staring up at the stranger, looking very confused and afraid.

He hadn't heard her enter the room. Ron threw off his clothes and speedily got into the boy's bed, in obvious excitement. She stood there in shock for a moment, not believing what she was seeing. She came to her senses and rushed over to the bed and instantly, without hesitation, grabbed the man's wrist, just as he was about to touch Simon's genitals. Ron looked up at her shocked. He said he had had a bit to drink and had lost his way when trying to find his own room. Jessy practically shouted at him, but conscious not to upset Simon, instructed him to get out of the bed and cover himself.

She continued to watch him closely until he was dressed. She could feel his embarrassment, at being so exposed to her. Jessy escorted him out of the room, checked on Simon, staying with him until he was dozing, then left, after locking the door. She knew very well what he had been up to. She wasn't born yesterday. She was just glad, that she had gone upstairs when she had, or it could have been a very different scene that she would have been witnessing.

What she had seen was bad enough.

After she had left the room, she went to find Simon's father. Edward was in his room, laying in bed. He couldn't sleep, so he was reading a book. When he heard a knock on his door, he waited a moment, to see if anyone would announce themselves. Jessy knocked again and said, "Sir, it's Jessy. I need to speak with you about something important."

He rolled out of bed and opened the door, after putting on a dressing gown, so she could enter his room. She related what had happened and her summation of what could have happened, if she hadn't seen him entering the room. He asked if anything else, untoward, had happened and if he had touched him anywhere, other than his head. She replied that he didn't have time because she had arrived, just before he had a chance to do anything. "Well then, no real harm done. I'll have a private word with Ron in the morning. Now you get off to bed, and thank you for letting me know."

Edward was disturbed to think that one of their circle of friends was a paedophile. He could tolerate all the other kinds of depravities that some of his friends possessed, such as the drugs, the orgies and the wife swapping and even the occasional bit of sadomasochism, that one or two of them obviously indulged in, due to the marks on them, that they tried hard to conceal, but even he had a limit. He didn't want to be associated with that kind of person. The papers would have a field day. More importantly, he could lose business, if people thought he allowed someone to abuse his only son.

He looked forward to telling Amelia tomorrow. She would go ballistic. He knew that she had slept with Ron on one occasion, a few months back. He had seen her enter his room when he had gone downstairs to fetch a glass of water. She was dressed in her pink fluffy baby doll nightwear. He had confronted her about it, the next morning and she had said that it was a moment of madness, that she regretted, because he talked to her like he was talking to a baby. It hadn't occurred to either of them at the time that he was attracted to children.

In the morning, before going into breakfast, Edward asked Ron if he could have a quiet word. "I understand that you wandered into my son's room last night?"

Ron tried to avoid eye contact with Edward. "Yes, on my return from the bathroom. I was confused. I didn't know which was my room. The housekeeper, walked in, just when I had pulled back the covers and got into bed. I'd had a bit to drink, I thought it was my room and was reaching out for whom I thought was Janet, so I had a bit of a shock when I noticed it was your boy."

"My housekeeper says you were in his bed and had been stroking his head, Ron."

"Yes, I could see that I had surprised him, so I was trying to soothe him. I know what it must have looked like to her. I can't apologise enough, Edward."

"Well, luckily for you, no harm was done, so I'll take no further action. Just make sure that it never happens again." Edward made a mental note, not to invite him to the house ever again and to make sure that the others closest to them were discretely made aware of his preferences.

Chapter Two

"Fabulous party, Edward. Your young son is very well mannered. I suppose you have big plans for his future."

"Yes John, I'd like him to come into the medical profession and possibly into my clinic once he's completed his exams, but that's some time off yet".

John coughs nervously, "When are you back in Switzerland, Edward? Um, my current girlfriend Helen, was asking me if I could fix up a consultation. I'd normally go through the usual channels, and wouldn't bring it up at a party, but I don't want Maxine to find out and need you to understand my situation. I don't want an expensive and messy divorce. More importantly, my position at the bank, wouldn't survive the publicity."

"No problem at all John, I'll be back in a couple of weeks. She can arrange to come and see me privately, one evening. Give her my private mobile telephone number and I'll set something up."

"That is very good of you, Edward. I need to keep her sweet, but don't want to spend a fortune on her. After all, I'm only with her for a bit of fun. It's not serious and I don't see it being a long term affair." Edward was thinking that this could be quite a lucrative arrangement if John had several 'bits of fun'.

Edward could see his wife approaching. "Ah! Hello darling. Let me introduce you to my wife, Amelia. Amelia, this is John, the new president at our bank in Switzerland."

Amelia beamed a smile. "A pleasure to meet you, John. I've just been speaking with your wife Maxine and arranged a tennis match at the club for when we fly over next. Maybe we could make it a doubles match?"

"That's very kind of you," replied John, "but I don't play. That's Maxine's 'thing'." Looking at Edward, meaningfully, he says, "She plays regularly, with her tennis coach Lewis."

This marriage, thought Edward, sounded very much like his own.

The alcohol was flowing and people had started to loosen up. John and Maxine, had to leave, in order to catch a late evening plane, back to Switzerland. When they'd left, Amelia dimmed the lighting and changed the music to something livelier, that they could all dance to.

Some of the regular invitees had started to openly flirt with each other's partners. Not all the guests wanted to be associated with the way the party appeared to be going. A few of the more discerning guests started to leave, at intervals, shortly after John and Maxine departed. They had a variety of excuses, from having to get up early the following morning, to checking up on one of their horses, who was in foal.

As the night wore on, Edward noticed that the flirting was becoming much more blatant. They were kissing and fondling each other on the dance floor and some had gone upstairs to find a bedroom, after getting overly excited.

Edward didn't get involved in the shenanigans, he was much more discrete and preferred to make himself look unobtainable. It appeared to him that women seemed to enjoy the challenge. When he finally gave in to their advances, he found them to be much more enthusiastic in the bedroom and wanted to fulfil his every need. It was as though they had won a prize. He preferred the 'hard to get' kind of reputation. What they didn't understand, was that they were playing his game.

As was usual, Simon was awoken, by the sound of his parents' friends roaming about, up and down the corridor, in the early hours. He could hear laughing and what sounded like an animal grunting in the room next to his. He couldn't imagine what was going on. He thought that they must have been playing a party game.

It was well after 4am, when the last of the guests had either gone home or retired to their rooms. Laughing, Amelia says, "I've told a few of the ladies that they are ageing really well, so I think that you may have a few extra clients quite soon." He could have told her, that he didn't need her assistance. He had plenty of clients but didn't see the harm in her thinking, she had some influence over his clientele.

"Are you going to join me in my room, Amelia?"

"Oh, darling, I'm absolutely exhausted. It's been a very long night and I really need my beauty sleep."

"I'll say goodnight then," he replied. Edward hadn't expected any other response. He knew she only stayed with him because he could give her a lifestyle that she revelled in and he had noticed her creeping off upstairs with Craig Delaware earlier, one of her regular partners at these affairs. He was probably making the most of her latest boob job. She thought that she had been able to hide her many indiscretions from him, but Edward was no fool. If she did ever threaten to divorce him, he would use her overt recklessness, against her and make sure that she didn't get her hands on his money.

She believed they had a lot of friends, but he understood, deep down, that it was because, being a renowned plastic surgeon, he could reinvent them, for a small fortune, into whoever they wanted to look like. He had worked on Amelia on numerous occasions. From the day he met her, even though she was very attractive, he was determining how he could transform her into his perfect woman. This had changed her in other unexpected ways though, which were not as pleasing and unfortunately, some of her less desirable traits had rubbed off on him too.

After the birth of their son, Amelia refused to have another 'body destroyer' as she had called Simon and brought in a nanny to care for him until he was 4 years old when she decided he could fend for himself. Amelia had never had that motherly connection with Simon like most other mothers appeared to have. She certainly wouldn't have even considered breastfeeding when he was a baby and instructed the nanny to give him baby formula. It was the nanny and Jessy that cuddled him and picked him up when he cried or he fell. The two of them saw his first steps and heard his first word. He had called the nanny 'Momma'. They had mentioned these events to Amelia, but she genuinely wasn't interested.

Amelia had become obsessed with looking younger and was constantly dieting and spent a small fortune on creams and lotions, in an effort to ward off any signs of ageing. As soon as she thought she was looking too old, she would ask Edward to carry out his magic on her. Just looking at her son made her feel old, so she had no interest in him whatsoever. In fact, if it wasn't for Edward wanting a son, she wouldn't have had him in the first place. Luckily, Jessy seemed to like him, so she was given the responsibility to take care of his day to day needs.

Not long after Simon was born, Amelia had booked herself into a private clinic for a hysterectomy, to make sure that she wouldn't have to wreak her body again and end up having another noisy child cluttering up the house. She had the operation, whilst Edward was away on business. On his return, Edward had asked her about the small scar on her stomach. She had told him what she had done and was surprised by his reaction. He had said that he wasn't bothered about having another child. He only needed one son to carry on the family name but would have preferred it, if she had consulted him beforehand. She answered that it wouldn't have made a difference, if he had wanted another child, she would still have gone ahead with the treatment. She said that the advantage of having the operation and coming off the birth control pill would mean that she wouldn't put any extra weight on now, as she wasn't consuming all that estrogen that would have made her fat. Edward had just smiled nonchalantly.

She thought she was on a higher plane than most, because she had a very rich and respected husband, which she believed, allowed her the pleasure of having anything she desired. They didn't see their old friends anymore, they only associated with the rich and famous, which suited Edward, as he had become everyone's 'must have' friend. He had been rewarded handsomely, not only very lucratively financially, but 'in kind' too with tickets to expensive events and the occasional new car, not to mention, he had engaged in quite a few very discrete affairs. So his marriage to Amelia suited both of them.

Chapter Three

When Simon reached the age of four, he was sent to prep school and as soon as it was legally possible, at the age of five, onto Boarding school. When he went home for the breaks from school, his parents were usually away on holiday. Simon spent his time with either the nanny or the housekeeper, who used to read books to him and play games. Their chats were about food or his train set, that his grandfather had sent him. When he was five, he would spend his time with Jessy and they would go on trips to the cinema or to the park. Like most boys of his age, he always insisted that she read him Thomas the Tank Engine when she put him to bed.

From the age of six, Simon started spending all his time, when not at school, with his grandfather, Maxwell, in either London or in Austria at one of his houses and once on holiday in New York, to visit the Neue Gallery in Manhattan. Although it had felt strange for Simon at the beginning, spending his holidays with a practical stranger, even though he had been told the man was his grandfather, they had liked each other straightaway. Gramps, as he preferred to be called, always had time for him and they would spend hours talking. When Simon was with his grandfather, they spent nearly every day either at one of the many splendid art galleries in

Austria, such as the Belvedere or the Leopold, which he adored, followed by luxurious afternoon teas, eating fancy cakes, taking picnics by the lake or picking grapes at his grandfather's vineyard. He'd even bought him his own horse, who he'd named Thomas and his grandfather had hired someone to teach him how to ride.

His grandfather expressed his views on the artworks that they went to see and, more importantly, asked Simon's opinion on what he felt about the different artwork and how he saw it. Throughout his short life, no one else, other than Jessy, had ever been interested in what he liked or didn't like and it piqued his interest in art. For fun, they used to make up funny stories about how they interpreted a particular painting. The days spent with his gramps were his most joyous and the only time he could remember, actually laughing and feeling truly happy and uncluttered.

As Simon was growing up, he became particularly interested in Gustaf Klimt's work. His grandfather started looking to purchase some other artwork that Simon had shown an interest in so that he could have his own collection. Some of the art that he did purchase remained in the galleries that they resided in, but they were still amongst his possessions. Simon was ecstatic. Not only did he have someone that talked with him and enjoyed his company, but he had been given lovely meaningful presents to keep for himself, something his parents had never indulged him with.

Edward had followed his father, Maxwell, into the medical profession. Maxwell had started his life as a doctor, then became a professor, then went on to specialise in tropical diseases. Unlike his father, Edward was more interested in prestige and money than improving people's lives. Although he thought he did that by making them look more aesthetically attractive.

Maxwell loved art and became an avid collector of fine art and rare wines. It was his second love. On his retirement, he could have made more money from his collections than he had from his profession, but as well as art, the need to help others, less fortunate than himself, had always been his ambition. He had inherited a large sum of money and some properties from his own family, so he was in a privileged position to keep and enjoy his art, as well as care for others.

He loved his grandson, but as a baby, only saw him on rare occasions. He was delighted, that as he'd become older, he had such an eye for art. From the early age of six, he showed such an obvious enjoyment in the opulence of the buildings that they visited and the colours and arrangement in the artwork, when they went to a gallery.

He would never understand his own son's self-absorption and his desperate need to impress others, who in his own eyes, were parasites, feeding off each other's perceived beauty and success. The media had helped in making them believe they were deities. His wife Amelia was even worse. In his opinion, she was the vainest most conceited woman on the planet. He felt that she had contaminated his son.

She was so afflicted, that she had even tried to seduce him to join the circus, that she called their circle of friends. They had had an almighty row when he was on his last visit to his son's house, for Simon's fourth birthday. Maxwell had told them both that they were taking themselves far too seriously and that they had developed into snobs of the highest order.

It meant nothing to Amelia and she would have forgiven him until he said it made them look unattractive and ugly. One thing that Amelia could not tolerate was being told she was ugly. Her whole life, since meeting Edward, was about how she was perceived by others, specifically in the looks department. She thought she was glamorous. The very thought of the word, ugly, made her physically cringe.

She had dedicated herself to looking attractive one hundred per cent of the time. She spent a great deal of money on designer clothes, expensive hair treatments and anything that made her look younger and more beautiful. She never came out of her bedroom suite without being immaculately turned out, dressed in designer gear and full makeup. These insults, made by Maxwell, were unforgivable and the last straw, as far as she was concerned.

Amelia had asked him to leave the house immediately. Maxwell was on his way home, as soon as he had packed his bags, even though Edward had tried to stop him, by saying that she would be fine once she had calmed down. Maxwell had said that he was glad to be leaving. They had not contacted each other since. Maxwell's only regret was that he could not see his grandson, due to the conflict between them.

He was, therefore, delighted when Edward had contacted him, two years later, to ask if he would like to see Simon. He was even more pleased when he suggested that Simon spent the holidays with him too. After the first holiday with his gramps, Simon insisted that he spent all his time with him and no one objected. In fact, it was a blessing to Amelia, who didn't want to be associated with having given birth to a child his age. It wouldn't have been good for the image that she wanted to portray.

Not long after Simon's first visit with his grandfather, the school were instructed by Amelia, to contact Maxwell with anything to do with Simon. They would let him know how well he was studying at his work at school, when the holidays were due and which flight he would be catching.

Each month, Maxwell would contact his son, Edward, to inform him of his son's progress at school, but this was the only conversation they had and it tended to be a very stilted dialogue. Edward only seemed interested in the positive things that Maxwell relayed back to him, so eventually, he didn't tell him of anything, that he believed, wasn't going as well. Maxwell never spoke with Amelia.

Chapter Four

Simon thought Prep school was okay, but the other boys didn't really like him, probably because he was shy and quiet and had started to develop a slight stammer, which only materialised at school. He was pushed a few times by Jason Kelly, who was a noisy individual, who liked to make a mess when they were painting or drawing. He even splattered red paint on Simon's picture for fun. All the other boys thought it highly hilarious, but Simon was devastated. The picture was of the zoo that he and Jessy had visited on his birthday and in his opinion, his best painting yet. He had wanted to give it to her for her birthday. When he did give it to her she had said what a wonderful picture he had painted her and that the red paint enhanced the painting. She would treasure it forever. Simon felt much better after that.

When he had moved onto boarding school, it became much harder for Simon. His father had told him that he had to study, study, study, or he would be a nobody in life and no one would want to be associated with a failure. The very thought of his gramps not wanting to be with him, drove him to his books at every opportunity. The teaching staff were amazed at his aptitude for studying but were concerned at his lack of interaction with the other children. Whilst the other boys indulged in the various sports available, he sat in a corner and read a book. The tutors tried everything to encourage him to join in, but he simply wasn't interested.

He had tried to play a game of rugby once but was relentlessly picked on by the other boys, who had fouled him at any opportunity. The games teacher Mr Chapman, didn't think anything untoward was happening. As far as he was concerned, playing rugby sorted out the 'wheat from the chaff.' In the dressing room, after the game, two of the boys had dunked his head in the toilet. The other boys all had a good laugh about it. They had also teased him in the showers about the size of his penis. The tutors were oblivious to the bullying and spoke with his father about their concerns about his lack of contact with the other boys. He told them not to be worried, he was the same at his age and he would eventually grow out of it.

Due to the taunts and isolation, he found it even harder to interact with the other boys at the school and eventually the boys started to call him 'simple Simon' because he couldn't talk to them without tripping over his words. But he was far from being simple. He was getting high grades for all his course work, which made his father extremely pleased. He took all the credit for his son's upbringing and would tell anyone who was interested in listening, that he was 'a chip off the old block', despite the fact, that he hardly had any interaction with Simon throughout his young life.

On his visits to his grandfather's, Simon never mentioned anyone from school. Maxwell queried his relationship with the other boys at school, but Simon told him that they were okay. Maxwell felt uneasy and contacted the school, who told him that everything was normal and that he had nothing to be concerned about.

When Simon reached sixteen years of age, his grandfather set up a bank account for him. This was to enable him to get any 'extras' that he may need for school. This was automatically topped up by direct debit, every month, with a thousand pounds. Simon already had a modest monthly allowance from his father, so he deposited the money that his grandfather gave him into a high-interest savings account every quarter. He told his gramps that the amount that he gave him, was far more than he needed, but was told that it was a way for him to avoid having to pay the taxman, when he eventually passed away. The very thought of his grandfather dying, made Simon shiver with anxiety.

As he progressed through school, the bullying became more frequent. His peers used to 'accidentally' trip him up and he would get pushed down the stairs. On a couple of occasions, he was attacked in the dormitory by a few of his antagonists, led by Harry Wentworth and his gang of four, Paul Butterworth, Tyler James, Archie Thompson and George Wallace.

Harry's father was 'high up' in the military, or so Harry had told the others, so he didn't see his son very often. When Harry was told that he would be going to Boarding School, he had said that he didn't want to go. His father told him he would have to 'tough it out'. Unfortunately, Harry had taken it out of context and always wanted to be in charge and keep the upper hand on others around him. He wanted to be just like his father and join the Army, so it was important to him to show that he could take control. Simon was an easy target to express his authority on. Simon was kicked in the back and punched in the stomach, but luckily the bruising was hidden. Harry threatened, that it would get much worse for him if he snitched.

During his middle years at school, Simon had been admitted to the school infirmary on numerous occasions with a fractured wrist and ankle, or cuts and bruises. He told his tutors that he had tripped over, or he had fallen down the stairs and this was only questioned by the school nurse once. The 'accidents' were so regular, that, in a perverse way, he had become used to the beatings and taunts, but he was even better at covering them up. He kept everything to himself.

The school nurse had suggested at the quarterly teachers meeting, that he was looked over at the city hospital, to make sure there was nothing more sinister going on with him. She said he had, by far, more referrals to her than any other student. After some discussion, the school made a decision to ignore any misgivings, based on their previous conversation with his father, where he had said that he was sent to that school, so they could make a man of him.

They had no evidence that Simon was being attacked and he hadn't accused anyone and besides, the parents were bringing in much-needed funds to the school. The last thing the school needed was a scandal. At the end of the day, a little potential bullying would make him a stronger man in years to come and after all, no real serious harm had been caused.

When Maxwell heard about the fractured wrist that Simon had obtained from a fall down the stairs, he grew more perplexed and contacted his son Edward to ask him to visit the school and enquire about his welfare. Edward agreed that he would when he and Amelia had returned from their holiday in Antigua.

Needless to say, by the time he returned from sunning himself on the beach, he had completely forgotten about the conversation. When Maxwell enquired about the response from the school, he lied and told him that he had spoken with the school and that there was nothing for them to worry about and that he was just a bit accident-prone. Edward thought that the conversation seemed to have appeased Maxwell, at least temporarily.

As Simon progressed through school, fortunately, the bullying did start to recede. His main protagonist, Harry Wentworth, was killed in a motorcycling accident after an all-night party. The school had been told that he and the driver of the bike had been drinking and smoking an illegal substance that they had been given by someone at the party. The boy who had been driving, drove into a tree, killing them both, instantly. When the school announced Harry's death at assembly, Simon couldn't help but inwardly smile and decided that maybe it was time for the others to suffer too. Everyone else at the school were now concentrating and working hard with their studies, to get through to their chosen Universities. After all the heartache that the others had caused him, Simon felt it was a good time to get some form of revenge.

Simon preferred to study at the local public library, rather than the one at school. He didn't feel threatened there and he could relax and concentrate on his work. Whilst he was packing up his revision work, he noticed a couple of boys outside the library. They were exchanging money, for what looked to him, to be drugs of some kind. An idea instantly started to formulate in his head. When he returned to school, he made the decision to contact the police anonymously and inform them that heroin was being distributed by Paul and Archie to the other students.

What he didn't know, was that Archie had been taking cocaine for the last year. When the police investigated, Archie was arrested and questioned after they found a stash at the back of his wardrobe. His parents appointed a solicitor, to look after their son's best interest, who asked the police, where they had obtained their information. The police said that they weren't at liberty to reveal their sources. They had enough evidence to charge him but would be more lenient toward him if he were to give them more useful information. During further questioning and after taking advice from his solicitor, Archie gave up the name of his supplier, who was further investigated, arrested and charged.

Following this, mayhem ensued at the school. Archie's parents were so appalled, they stopped his allowance immediately and had to come to an agreement with the school, to prevent him from being expelled. Six months later, a new gymnasium was being built at the school.

Paul and Tyler became much more cautious and it was obvious, from their demeanour, that they were also having issues at home. Other children in the school were questioned, including Simon. There were a few cautions, but no further arrests, until eventually it quietened down.

The school changed too and became much more vigilant to the comings and goings of its residents. Because Simon had been questioned, along with the other boys at the school, no one suspected him of being the informer. Simon thought that once he had his revenge, he would feel pleased, but he didn't feel anything.

Six months later Archie committed suicide. On further investigation, by the school and the police, they found, what could have been construed as, threatening emails from a locally known drug dealer. According to his friends, he had told them that he thought he was being followed. However, none of them had taken him seriously. Although, on reflection, they said he had become more withdrawn lately. The tutors were interviewed, but all of them said, that they hadn't noticed any change in him. Because of the upset earlier in the year, it wasn't difficult to understand why he had been targeted. The police decided they had enough to arrest the dealer, get him locked up and take him off the streets, at least for a while. Unfortunately, the prosecution didn't agree that they had enough evidence. It was mostly circumstantial and they didn't believe they could make it stick. Remarkably, the accused had never been in court before or even had a caution.

Chapter Five

Because of Simon's high marks at school, his grandfather, as a reward for his hard work, decided to buy Simon a new car. Edward, on the other hand, decided to take Simon to his workplace in Switzerland, to show off his own expertise, in an effort to encourage him, to potentially work with him in the future. He emphasised how improved the person he was operating on looked, how grateful they were and how lucrative it could be for him. He would never have to worry about bills and expenses in his lifetime.

Simon wasn't interested in the money that he could earn and he really didn't want to work with his father. He was the very last person that he wanted to be like. Simon studied well, as his father had insisted, so he appreciates the work that his father had carried out and the reconstructions he had created. They very nearly could have been classified as works of art, but they were all very similar. Although he could follow what his father was doing, as he had read and studied the books at the library, in readiness for advancing onto University, he had no real interest in the kind of medical procedures that his father performed and it wasn't the profession that he wanted to move into.

Simon, was in the library, as always, carrying out some research for his latest school project, when he met Dawn Edwards, who was supposed to be studying too. She sat down next to him and started to try and talk to him about a party she was going to at the weekend.

He didn't pay any attention at first. She was just an annoyance.

Then he looked up from his books. She had big brown eyes and light brown hair that was highlighted with what looked, to Simon, as being gold twinkles. Her eyes sparkled whilst she talked. Simon couldn't take his eyes off her and was amazed that she had chosen to speak to him, not that there were many other people to talk with, in the library, on a Monday lunchtime.

He made an effort to be at the same desk, at the library at the same time, every day. She didn't come back for the following couple of weeks and he couldn't help but feel disappointed. However, the following week, a little later than before, in she strolled.

This time, he decided to talk to her. "How was your party the other week?" He asked.

She looked up, smiling and said, "Which one? I'm always out partying." She could see he was shy and a little embarrassed, but reasonably good looking, not the usual type of boy she was attracted to, but she was amused by the way he looked at her and blushed. She asked him about his family and interests and was impressed by his background and more importantly his wealth. "Why not come with me to the next one?"

"Yes, I'd like that."

"It's a date then," she said.

They arranged to meet at 9pm outside the library on Friday night.

The date was unremarkable and Dawn thought he had very little experience with girls, but he obviously had money and went to a posh school, not a public academy like her. The one thing that she was amazed at, was that he didn't try and 'jump her', which made it an easy choice when he asked her out again. She liked the way he opened doors for her and fetched her a drink. He was so polite and she knew having him with her, impressed her friends. One of her friends had asked her, if she could ask him, to introduce her, to one of his rich friends. Dawn had instantly said that she would, but not until she'd been out with him a few times first. She had no intention of asking him. She didn't want her friends potentially spoiling her good fortune.

He was so naive that she could manipulate him to do what she wanted, even though he bored her rigid. She couldn't discuss popular music or the latest trends with him and found it difficult to find anything in common to talk about. He would pick her up from outside the library, in his new silver Mercedes and off they would go to a fancy restaurant of her choosing or to her favourite clothes shop, where he would treat her to something lovely and expensive. She would tell all her friends about the expensive dinners and clothes that he bought her, in an effort to make them envious.

He was never invited to her home. Dawn created a story of her living in a typical semidetached house in suburbia. She told him that her father was sick and they couldn't disturb him. This was true, to some extent. Being an alcoholic, he was always drunk and incapacitated. Her mother worked at the local launderette, so they didn't have much money. Because her mother worked all the hours she could get, the flat tended to look like a refuge tip. This was more ubiquitous when her father was on a bender and throwing, what little furniture they had, against the flimsy walls, or putting his fist through them. She really didn't want Simon to know how she lived. In fact, she had told the same story to most of her friends too.

She'd never had it so good, and he'd never even made a move on her, apart from a goodnight kiss. Normally, after a night out, she'd have been in the back of a car or around the back of the club, with her knickers at her ankles, after too many lager and limes, whilst the one night stand was thrusting away like a steam engine until he had satisfied himself. She was now drinking gin and tonic with a slice of lemon and trying hard at acting prim and proper, being dropped off at the library, after a peck on the lips and waiting for him to drive away and then phoning for a taxi to take her home. She had told him that she lived close to the library, so he never questioned her.

Simon was besotted. She was his first girlfriend and he'd already decided that she was the one for him. Dawn, after discovering who his parents were having googled them on the internet, before their first date and was over the moon that she had landed on her feet. She was determined to milk this one for as long as she could.

The only time the two of them didn't meet, was when he went to his gramps for the holidays, or he was engrossed in his studying. Dawn never went on holiday with him, because she told him that she recognised that he needed to be free to visit his gramps to do the things they liked to do together. She also said that it was good for their relationship to have some space, from time to time, so that they didn't get into a rut.

Although he tried to reason with her that it would be okay for the three of them to get together, she was adamant. She knew he wasn't happy about this, so made sure that she gave him a good send-off when they were due to be separated, by showing him how good she was at getting him aroused and then pleasuring him. She told him that it was something for him to think about whilst he was away and something for him to look forward to on his return.

Even though he wanted her to meet his gramps, he didn't force the issue, in case she decided to leave him for pressurising her. After all, he thought, she was a free spirit and really turned him on.

Whilst he was away, Dawn was out enjoying herself at the local nightclub in her new expensive designer finery. She was meeting other men and having a ball. Knowing that she would be bored to death on Simon's return, she was throwing herself into making the most of his absence. Her friends warned her that if her antics got back to Simon he would finish with her, but she just laughed and said she would deny everything and besides, she could make him believe anything she said. He trusted her implicitly. Some of her friends stopped being as friendly with her. They didn't want to be tarred with the same brush. She might be dressed to the nines in her posh clothes, but she was acting like a slut.

Chapter Six

Although Simon excelled at all his classes, when it came to having to sit for his final exams, he suffered from extreme anxiety. He was so afraid of the repercussions from his father and the disappointment from his gramps if he failed. He tried very hard to conceal it from others. After all, he had plenty of experience at hiding his feelings, but this only heightened his feeling of dread. Simon tried to discuss this with Dawn, but he could tell that she wasn't really interested. He suggested that they don't see one another until he had completed them. She pretended to be disappointed, but inwardly she was ecstatic. He had given her the freedom to enjoy herself again and let her hair down.

During the exams, he became so inwardly upset, that his writing, if he managed to put pen to paper, became illegible. When this happened, he didn't sleep and couldn't eat properly, worrying about his next exam. At the beginning of his exams, he was so overwhelmed, that all he could hear were the whispers from the other students, "simple Simon" being repeated over and over again in his head and he struggled to write anything other than scrawl and doodles, whilst daydreaming, in an effort to try and calm himself. To others, he looked like he was concentrating on his exam.

By the time he steadied himself, he reasoned that he could probably have attempted and aced the exam. Unfortunately, by the time he arrived at this point in his thought process, it was all over and the invigilators were collecting the papers. All he'd actually managed to complete was to write his details on the front cover.

No one looked at his papers, after all, he was a grade-A student in the class and he'd breezed through his mock exams. The papers were sent off to the examining board with everyone else's, so no one suspected that he hadn't completed them.

He knew that he's failed all his examinations, even though he probably would have known most of the answers. He can hear his father's rants in his head, and his gramps, would be bitterly disappointed in him, so he decided not to reveal anything until the results were out. There was only one exam that he was actually looking forward to.

His art examination, was not like other exams. The exam format was just like a series of normal lessons, but without interruptions from the teacher or other students. He could get on with his work in peace, bringing his own ideas to life. Simon's favourite class was art, so for his examination, he decided, influenced by his father's work, that he would reconstruct his favourite Gustav Klimt work and design a 3D structure.

Instead of copying the work, he would create his own interpretation of the art. He spends time experimenting with different medium to construct his artwork and discusses, with his tutor, Mr Fredrick, different ideas, on how to present it. When he contacts his gramps, he is very excited about his artwork. Maxwell is thrilled. He hasn't heard the boy so animated in a long time and praises him for his hard work and excellent idea.

Three weeks before the end of the art examination, however, the Principle at the school asks to see Simon, to inform him that his grandfather had died, suddenly, of a heart attack. Simon looks blankly at him and feels like the world has just crumbled around him. Outwardly, it appears that he doesn't care. He has become so adept at hiding how he feels. The Principle can't believe the lack of emotion, that he is witnessing and dismisses him back to his class.

His father decides that this is a good time to take him out of school. After all, he only has his art exam left to complete, which will be of no use to him in later life, as he informs Simon. He arranges for a colleague, Brian, to pick him up from school and drop him off at home. The school made separate arrangements for his luggage to be delivered. Brian had successfully assisted Edward with an operation on a woman called Barbara a few weeks before, who had been introduced to Edward by another friend of his at a party. Edward was quite taken by her and had flirted with the idea of bedding her sometime in the future, but he needed to find out more about her relationship with her husband.

Brian had mentioned to Edward, that he was planning on visiting some friends in the vicinity, close to where Simon went to school, whilst they were having lunch earlier that day, so when Edward had asked him if he would pick up his son, after his visit and drop him off at home, he had happily agreed.

Brian is surprised that Edward or Amelia are not fetching their son from school but concludes that Simon mustn't have been very close with his grandfather, or a family member would have collected him. He was curious to find out a little more about Edward, from his son. Even though he'd worked with Edward for a couple of years now, he doesn't know him. All the time that they've worked together, they had never talked about his personal life, until Edward's father had died and even that conversation had been very brief. The only other conversation that he had with him usually, was about medical procedures. Brian had the impression that Edward thought that because he owned the business, he was a class above him. Edward paid him well, so he couldn't complain.

Simon is so upset, but again, can't express how he feels, because no one else would understand. He's distraught about his grandfather's death and upset that he hasn't managed to complete his artwork. Now he's leaving school a complete failure. His only relief is that he won't see the disappointment in his gramps' eyes. Simon has never met Brian, but the school had informed him that his father had arranged for him to be taken home.

Brian tries to start a conversation with him, but this tends to be very awkward when he only gets one or two-word replies and he is pleased when Simon asks him if he will drop him off at the shops nearby. On his way home, Brian decides that he is just like his father, closed and unapproachable.

Simon spends a few hours wandering the streets, looking in shop windows, but not really seeing anything. He calls into a coffee shop and sips at his cappuccino, occasionally nibbling at his lemon drizzle cake, whilst watching the world go by. He isn't looking forward to seeing his parents. Even though they don't know his results yet, he feels guilty that he has let them down, by failing at school and won't be able to go into the medical profession, as his father had wanted him to. Eventually, he makes his way to a taxi rank and goes home.

On his return, he discovers from someone called Lydia that his parents have gone away for a few days to meet up with some friends and that Jessy and Colin have left, due to his illness. Simon wasn't concerned that his parents were away, but was upset that no one had informed him that Jessy and Colin had left.

Chapter Seven

Two days after Maxwell's death, Jessy's husband, Colin, who is employed as the gardener/handyman at the house, was diagnosed with cancer. They decide that they will both have to hand in their notice and leave their employment at the house. Amelia is more upset at the inconvenience that it will cause her to find a new housekeeper, than feeling any empathy for their plight. Even though they know of their monetary position, unsurprisingly, neither Amelia nor Edward consider helping them financially for the service and loyalty that they have given them over the years.

Jessy's sister, who lives alone, offers to take them both in to live with her, knowing they don't have enough money to purchase somewhere of their own. It is a bit cramped for space, but they would manage, and it was close to the hospital, for Colin's appointments. Regardless of her own personal circumstances, Jessy still worried about Simon. However, now that Simon is much older, she wasn't as concerned as she might have once been.

It doesn't take Amelia long to replace them. She contacted the employment agency, as soon as she heard about Colin's demise. She asks for a part-time handyman, who lives in the village, to come up to the house once a week to tidy up the garden and carry out any repairs that might be needed on the house, but requires a live in housekeeper/cook. She employs a semi-retired local man called Jim, who appears to be very capable and happy with the working hours.

She interviews Lydia Newland, who she discovers is a widow and has no close family or offsprings, who looks like she'd be an ideal housekeeper. She appears compliant and will not question Amelia's orders.

Lydia is relieved to have been given this job. She had been on the books at the employment agency for months. Every time she had been given a job, she had been asked to leave after a couple of weeks. The feedback that she had been given from the agency was that she wasn't friendly enough and people found her hard to converse with. She knew she was quiet, but did as she was told and thought she carried out a decent job. She hadn't been employed as a companion, so couldn't comprehend why she couldn't retain a position.

When she came to work for Mr and Mrs Harrington, she instantly knew she would fit in. She wasn't expected to chat. In fact, Mrs Harrington had given her a list of written instructions on her arrival. She was told that she must not do anything more, or anything less than had been stipulated in the instructions. She was told that she shouldn't bother her unless something very important occurred and it was imperative that she needed to be informed. She was allowed her own time, which she could spend doing whatever she wanted. She had always had a very regimented way of life. She spent her time knitting sweaters or crocheting blankets to give to charity. She ordered her wool from the same supplier to be delivered every month. She went for a walk once a week to the park and listened to The Archers on the radio. This job suited her lifestyle, perfectly.

Edward tells Amelia that Simon would be better off left alone, to come to terms with everything that had happened, which is one of the reasons that they chose to be with their new friends on Simon's return from school. The other reason was that Edward rather liked Barbara, with whom he had had a brief encounter with earlier on in the year, at one of the many parties that he attended and after some discrete enquiries, had discovered, that like most of their friends, they liked to indulge in the occasional affairs. He had carried out some work on enhancing her derrière, which seemed to be the trend this year. He never thought he would like such voluptuous looking behinds. He usually was attracted to the very slim streamlined body. He remembered how it had made him feel when he was fondling his handiwork after the surgery. It made him feel physically excited just thinking about it.

When they arrive at their friends', Edward was immediately attracted to Barbara and couldn't tear his eyes from her and it appeared that the feeling was mutual. Her husband Jeremy was openly flirting with Amelia. Against all his usual cautiousness, he recklessly asks Barbara if she is interested in a little light entertainment. She laughs saying that is exactly what they were hoping for when they invited them and she puts her hand on his obvious erection and gives him a gentle squeeze.

She grasps his hand and they head off upstairs, literally tearing each other's clothes off with their eyes. Amelia is happy with the arrangement but totally surprised at her husband, who she believes never has sex with anyone but her, which admittedly, nowadays, wasn't very often. She is definitely seeing a new side to her husband.

When they are upstairs, Edward rapidly unzips his trousers, pulls up her skirt and practically rips off her pants and instantly enters her. He is so excited that he feels like King Kong. He can feel his penis throbbing in anticipation. He drives into her as if his life depended upon it. Normally a considerate lover, he is only thinking about his own satisfaction. Barbara has never felt so exhilarated by a man's need to possess her.

After their first frenzied coupling, they both take time caressing each other until they are both ready to start all over again. Edward can't remember ever feeling so fulfilled before and found it difficult to control himself. It was important to him, to make sure she was satisfied before he exploded into her again. He had never experienced sex like this with Amelia.

Jeremy and Amelia stayed downstairs and she is amazed at his stamina. She has never had sex in so many different positions in such a short amount of time. They had utilised every surface of the room. He bent her over the table, had thrown her on the sofa, pinned her to the floor, taken her from behind against the wall and repeatedly pumped his endless fluids into her, while she came and then came again. She was totally satisfied and feeling exhausted. She can't remember having so many multiple orgasms. She comes to the conclusion that he must be on Viagra.

Whilst at breakfast, on the second day of their visit, Jeremy and Barbara ask them both if they would contemplate a foursome, but Edward said that it wasn't really his thing. Amelia, for once, agreed with her husband. Personally, she would have jumped at the chance, but she thought that

Edward was much too prudish to participate in something like that. After all, she thought, this was the first time that he'd had sex with someone else. Maybe, he would become a bit more experimental as time went by and be more interesting. Barbara and Jeremy laugh and say that it's okay. They were just putting the idea out there.

Barbara asks if they would like to extend their stay, as their other plans to go to a couple of their friends, Diane and Liam's, had been postponed, due to an unexpected visit from their daughter. They were supposed to be going to a photographic exhibition of Diane's, but could go to see her work at another time of the year.

Later that day, Edward and Amelia decide that they would like to stay for a couple of days longer. They didn't want to spoil their stay, by even thinking about going back home just yet. Edward can't get enough of Barbara's body and Amelia couldn't remember feeling this sated before in her life. They felt like addicts in constant need of a fix.

Chapter Eight

When they arrive home, after their extra-long weekend away, Edward and Amelia are reminded by Lydia, that Simon is in the house. She tells them that he isn't eating all his food and he hadn't been out of his room since his return home. She mentions that she called the doctor while they were away, who had prescribed him medication to help him cope with his anxiety and to help him sleep. She told them that she had heard him having nightmares since his return home and hoped that they didn't mind her making the call to the doctor. They assured her that it was the right thing to have done. During their time away, they had forgotten all about the death of Edward's father and Simon hadn't entered their heads, but neither of them felt even a twang of remorse.

Leaving Simon alone suited Amelia down to the ground. She would have no idea what to say to him and besides, she thinks, she is far too busy with her own life, to be spending her precious time, pampering a miserable boy. Edward did feel a little sympathy for his son but felt that he wasn't the correct person who could help him through his grief and suggested to Amelia that perhaps a counsellor would be the answer. She says she will deal with it, then instantly forgets, when one of her friends rings her up for a chat about a new spa opening nearby.

Simon has become lethargic and listless, spending all his time in his room. For the first couple of weeks, he leaves his meals, half-eaten, outside his room for Lydia to retrieve. She is much less friendly than Jessy had been, but she appears to fit well into the household. He watches her while she busies herself around him. She keeps herself to herself, carrying out the tasks she had been told to do, then leaves him alone.

Not long after his grandfather's death, Maxwell's solicitor had sent a letter to Simon giving details of his grandfather's will, which leaves everything to him, but the inheritance is no replacement for his gramps, and he feels as though his whole world has stopped.

When Lydia gave him his mail, he read it and then waited for her to leave. He put the letter into his desk, which was situated under the window of his room and locked it.

Whilst he's laying in bed, wide awake at 3am, he can hear voices calling to him. "Simple Simon. You're nothing but a failure. We are going to get you. We're watching you!"

Later that morning, Amelia discusses with Edward how they can get him to come out of his room. "After all, it's been long enough now Edward, it's time he started to get out and about and stop wallowing. He can't stay in there forever."

"What happened regarding the counsellor?" Edward asked.

"No help whatsoever," she replied. In fact, she had forgotten all about it.

Amelia is irked that Simon is in his room feeling sorry for himself and she decides that she needs to escalate his recovery. She asks Lydia to look for his mobile phone when she next takes in his lunch. She picks it up surreptitiously from his bedside cabinet and passes it on to Amelia, as instructed. Amelia browses through his meagre amount of contacts and briefly through his text messages, which are few. They all appear to be from someone called Dawn and it's obvious from the content, that they are seeing each other.

After some discussion between Amelia and Edward, they decide to ask Dawn to visit, to see if she can coax him out of his room. They text her and arrange to send a car to pick her up. When she arrives, through the electric gates, she's taken aback at the enormous house and the expensive decorations. As she walks through the door, Edward is complaining about the gate's mechanism, squeaking, to who appeared to be the handyman. *Wow!* she thinks. *This is how I want to live.* She knew he came from money, but this was something else. The house was immaculate. There were, what looked like, original antique pieces around the house and very stylish furnishings. This was a completely different way of living than what she was used to.

She had been brought up on a notoriously rough council estate, on the tenth floor, in a block of flats. They were lucky if the lifts moved, never mind squeaked. She decides that she can put up with the tedium of seeing Simon, to get this kind of lifestyle. She is mesmerised by Simon's mother, who, in her eyes, is absolutely beautiful and so young looking.

Amelia and Edward, on the other hand, can't believe that he has been seeing her for so long. She is definitely not the sort of girl that they want their son to be seeing, especially, now that he was living under their roof. They could tell that she was trying to put on a more refined accent, which they thought was amusing. It was obvious that she was not from the kind of family that they would want their son to be associated with.

Although they didn't want her in their house longer than necessary, she was their last resort, at getting him to come out. Unfortunately, she couldn't get him to leave his room either but did manage to get him to talk, which was more than anyone else had managed, but this meant, to Amelia's disgust, that she would have to come back again.

Luckily Edward was in Switzerland, working, so he didn't have to deal with the unpleasantness. Amelia, organised the days for Dawn to visit, but was always conveniently out, so didn't have to converse with the girl.

Dawn had tried to talk with Simon but didn't know where to start. She told him about a new shop that had opened that she wanted them to visit and about a new restaurant that had opened on the high street, but when she didn't get any response, decided it would be more interesting to explore her surroundings. Simon was watching her lips move but was not comprehending anything she was saying. He had switched off. He was back with his gramps, in New York, soaking up the atmosphere, or eating Sachertorte at one of the many coffee houses in Vienna, drinking a hot chocolate and discussing the latest acquisitions at the art gallery.

On most of Dawn's visits to the house, she spent it mooching around. She nosied through cupboards and drawers. Her favourite time in the house though was looking through Amelia's bedroom suite, trying on her clothes and jewellery. She had to be careful though so that she didn't alert Lydia to what she was doing. She knew which day she went to the park and what time The Archers would be on the radio, so usually played 'dressing up' during those times.

On one occasion, she found a beautiful ring at the back of one of her jewellery boxes that looked like diamonds. She popped it in her jacket pocket. Amelia had so much, she was certain that she wouldn't miss it. Dawn was tempted to take more but didn't want to chance her luck. After all, she would inherit all of this, if she played her cards right and managed to get Simon to put another ring on her finger.

On one of her social calls, she told Lydia that if she wanted to go out, she would look after things at the house. Lydia had noticed that the local cinema was going to be screening an old black and white film of Citizen Kane, that afternoon that she would really like to see. With Mrs Harrington being away for the day, it would be a good opportunity for her to go and see it. She had no reason to mistrust Dawn, as she believed that the Harrington's wouldn't have asked her to the house otherwise. She reasoned that Mrs Harrington wouldn't be any the wiser if she spent some leisure time in town.

With Lydia out of the way, Dawn decided to take a bath in Amelia's bathroom and use the expensive-looking products that were at the side of the enormous bathtub. She felt like a million dollars, languishing, with her body surrounded by a mass of sweet-smelling bubbles. After she had towelled herself dry and dressed, she heard a car in the drive. She hurriedly tidied up the room and ran into Simon's room. She looked out of the window to see a delivery van. She breathed a sigh of relief. She had thought that it might have been Amelia or Lydia returning home.

She dashed downstairs to receive the parcel from the delivery man and then ran back upstairs to Amelia's bathroom, to clean up the room, as best she could. On a previous visit, she had found a cupboard that had sheets and towels in it. She replaced the towels and then tossed the wet ones into Simon's dirty laundry basket. Although she had enjoyed the experience immensely, she decided that she wouldn't risk it again.

She went to see if she could get any kind of response from Simon, but he was still away with the fairies, so she went from room to room to see if she could find anything interesting. When she entered the study, she started to look through the desk but found nothing of real interest. She was astounded at the cost of the bills they were paying and the amount of money they appeared to spend, according to the bank statements that she glanced through. Her parents could live for a year on what they spent in a month, on food alone.

There was a safe in both Edward and Amelia's rooms, but try as she might, she couldn't find the combination codes anywhere. She thought that they probably knew the security codes off by heart, or maybe kept the codes on their computers. She soon became bored and gave up looking.

Lydia had really enjoyed her rare afternoon out. She had watched the film, eating a small tub of vanilla ice cream and had even indulged in a small bucket of popcorn, which was so unlike her. She had felt unfettered for the first time in a very long time and was already planning her next escapade. By the time she was on the bus, on her way back to the house, any thoughts of reliving the afternoon had gone from her mind. She was already thinking about what she was going to prepare for the evening meal.

When she eventually arrived home, Dawn was sitting in the hall with her coat on. Lydia was mortified. "I'm so sorry if I've kept you waiting."

"I've only just come downstairs. Its fine," lied Dawn. Lydia asked if Simon required anything, but Dawn said that he was okay. She hadn't actually checked in on him, since she had the scare with the delivery man, but assumed he'd be alright. She'd been in the lounge, drinking some of their scotch, before realising the time, and putting on her coat, a couple of minutes before Lydia was due home.

Chapter Nine

Maxwell, at his request, hadn't had a formal funeral. He had given his body for research and asked for any remains to be sent on to the crematorium for disposal, without ceremony. He hadn't been a religious man and believed if you had had a good life, once you were dead, there was nothing to mourn.

Edward wasn't upset at his father's death. Although it was no surprise to Edward, that Amelia was angry that they were not included in his will. Neither had any idea what was in his will or how much he actually owned, or even, how much he had bequeathed. Edward had more than enough money to do what he wanted to do at the moment, so he wasn't going to let Amelia know that he believed his father had been a very wealthy man.

Maxwell's solicitor had told them that their son was the only inheritor, but he wouldn't disclose anything else, so she told Edward that they needed to be amenable to Simon during the next few months, to see if they could find out if there was anything worth having.

During the first month after Maxwell's death, Amelia intermittently starts taking his meals up to his room, with Lydia, stopping at his bedside to tell him about the exploits of the people she spent time with. All her talk went way over

Simon's head. He didn't know these people and he didn't want to know them. The voices he had started to hear, were telling him, that she was trying to catch him out so that she could tell the others how to kill him. He decided, that to defend himself, he would not react to her in the slightest and certainly would not converse with her.

This was the only time that he could remember his mother actually trying to have a conversation with him, which made him even more suspicious. He would have to be careful. After only two days, Amelia realises that she is getting no response from him and only spends fifteen to twenty minutes talking, every other day, then once a week, then decides to give up trying altogether. In her opinion, he is a strange and unsettling character and concluded that she didn't like him, even if he was her son.

As instructed at the beginning of her employment, Lydia sorts through the mail and distributes it. When his exam results finally come through, she doesn't realise what they are, when she leaves his mail by the side of his bed. He is not surprised that he has failed all of his examinations subjects and has not graduated. Simon believes everyone around him has conspired to get him and they have made him fail on purpose. He puts the results under his pillow.

Later that day, the housekeeper and his mother are at the side of his bed, discussing something to do with his evening meal. When there is more than one person in his room, he starts to become upset, so he completely shuts down his thoughts, so they can't get into his head. Once he's alone again, the voices are telling him that they are all watching him. He takes the results letter from under his pillow and throws it on the floor in a pique of defiance.

After over a month of coaxing, at different times, from both Dawn and Amelia, finally, he emerges from his room. He announces that he is going out, but doesn't tell Amelia where to, or for how long. Amelia is very pleased. "It's a step forward, from him being ensconced in his room, like a hermit, making the place look untidy," she says to Edward, over the phone.

Simon's made a decision that he can't stay in this house any longer, because it's too dangerous. He goes to the airport, buys a standby ticket and he flies to Austria. On his arrival, he goes to his grandfather's house, changes his clothes and arranges a visit with his grandfather's solicitors.

He spends some time going through the details of the will. He identifies where the properties that he has inherited are and highlights them on a map and then lists the paintings that he now owns, in order of his own preference.

When he doesn't appear back at the house, after a couple of days, Edward tries to contact him on his mobile phone. He receives a text back, saying that he has gone away for a few days. He'll be back soon, but doesn't tell him where he is.

Whilst cleaning his room, Lydia discovers his exam results from under the bed. She passes them onto Amelia. On Edward's return from work, she is beside herself with anger at her son's failure. Edward is extremely disappointed and feels embarrassed that his son has let them down so badly. He can't understand how this has happened. He was doing so well at school. Everyone had told him so.

"Amelia, I have made a decision about Simon. I think he is old enough to look after himself from now on. I think we should suggest that he sets himself up in a flat somewhere, away from London. Can you imagine what our friends will think if they knew?"

"I don't mind where you send him Edward, I can't believe that he's failed ALL his examinations. The embarrassment and humiliation of it all. I am not going to tell any of our friends if they ask and I do not expect you to either. As far as I am concerned, we don't have a son anymore." To keep her calm, Edward agrees with her.

Amelia is far from calm though and immediately sends a text to Simon, to say, that they know about his results and they are ashamed of him. On his return, he will have to find somewhere else to live, preferably as far away from them as possible.

Chapter Ten

On his return from Austria, Simon arranges to meet with Dawn. He feels much more positive after his conversation with the solicitor and the voices have been quieter too. With his own money and that of his grandfather's, he can now afford to travel, at short notice, to anywhere in the world, if the need arises and he can provide for himself and Dawn without any help from others.

Simon was glad to have left his education behind. At 19 years of age, he knows, that he can do what he wants. He tells Dawn that his parents have disowned him and he wants them both to go and live in Austria, somewhere where they would be alone and comfortable.

He adds, that the last thing he wants, is a life like his parents.

Dawn looks at him as though he has been speaking in alien tongues. She is shocked to hear that he has fallen out of favour with his parents and she panics. She tells him, that he hasn't spoken to her properly for weeks, then he expects her to, 'up sticks' and go away with him, at the click of his fingers. "You've completely lost the plot, Simon."

She blurts out, that whilst he's been away 'finding' himself, she has been seeing someone else. She doesn't mention that she's been two-timing Simon for over six months.

John is married, but that has made it more exciting and it was convenient for both of them since they both had partners. John was far more fun. She had met him when he had been on a stag night at the nightclub. On numerous occasions, he had told her that he loved her, though admittedly, this was usually when they were both in bed at the motel. She was hoping, that if she left Simon, John would leave his wife for her.

Although she has no idea how wealthy he is, she believes that Simon must have a reasonable amount of money, but can't imagine living with him, far away from her friends in another country, where she couldn't speak the language. They had nothing in common. He bored her and the very thought of living with him fills her with horror.

She makes the decision to end their relationship, after all, she won't be mixing with the gentry, now that the link has been broken with his parents. The way she looked at it, he'd already bought her the car she wanted and she has the diamond ring from his mother's house and she had lots of lovely things that he had bought her. She now wanted to enjoy herself. "I think we need a break, Simon. I've been feeling unhappy with our relationship for some time."

Simon is not crestfallen at her decision and discovers that perhaps, he doesn't love her as much as he thought he did. There had been a lot of changes in his life recently and he comes to the conclusion that, in the scheme of things, she isn't at the top of his list of priorities.

Dawn can't wait to see John. Now that she is free of Simon, there is nothing stopping them from being together. However, the excitement of the affair dulls, once John finds out that she's left Simon. John never thought of Dawn as anything, but an easy lay. She was adventurous and exciting in bed, but just a tart he had picked up and he had no intention of ever leaving his wife. He tells her that it's been fun, but it was time to move on. Dawn can't believe that he's finishing their relationship. She thought she was something special to him.

After some contemplation, she tries to contact Simon, in the hope of getting back with him. She had come up with a lie, about how she felt he had pushed her away, after his grandfather's death. She had said the things she said to upset him because she was hurt and she hadn't had an affair. She hadn't meant any of it and truly loved him. When she tries to contact him, however, he does not answer her calls. She realises, that it's too late to go back to how things were and she's really messed up. How could she have been so naive. She can't believe that she fell for John's lies. However, if John thought he could treat her that way, he was in for a sharp awakening.

Dawn knew where John lived. She had seen his address on the register at the motel. She put a pair of scanty panties into an envelope with a note saying, 'See you later, darling. Can't wait to see you again, lover.' She sent it to his address, with his name on the front and put an s after the Mr.

On Simon's return from Austria, one of his tasks was to locate and contact Jessy, so after his talk with Dawn, he went to visit her at her sister's. He asks after her husband and she tells him that his treatments are going as well as can be expected. After she has told him about what she is occupying herself with, he hands her a cheque for £500,000. She says she can't possibly take it, but Simon is insistent, saying he has inherited a great deal of money and he wants her to have it. She is moved to tears. She can't believe his generosity. Simon says that if she needs anything else then she must not hesitate to contact him and he would be happy to help her.

When she asked him why he wanted to help them, he told her that she had been more of a mother to him than his actual mother ever had been, or ever would be and more importantly, she had cared for him when he needed her the most. She had replied that she would always be there for him. He apologised that it had taken him so long to come and see her, but he hadn't been in a good place after his grandfather died. She told him that she understood perfectly and hoped that he would be able to find peace, as time went by.

Chapter Eleven

At his father's suggestion and mother's insistence, Simon decides to purchase his own house. After searching the internet, he finds a house he likes the look of, in Leeds, West Yorkshire. He's looking forward to a new start, somewhere fresh, away from his parents. It's a vibrant city, with plenty to do to occupy him. It's also another bolt hole when he needs to avoid the voices.

He notices a few unread messages from Dawn on his mobile phone, but deletes them without reading them. She is truly now in his past. He couldn't believe he'd been with her all this time. She was greedy and vain. The voices had told him that she was just like his mother, so on reflection maybe that was what had attracted him to her. He doesn't want Dawn to contact him again, so he decided to buy some new throw away phones. That would stop her and his unknown pursuers from knowing where he was.

After he makes the decision to move, he travels to Leeds to view the house he'd seen online and pays for it in cash. It is perfect for his needs. It's a traditionally build detached house, with a beautiful garden, situated in a secluded area, but not too far away from the city centre. The house has been well maintained and there is enough distance between the houses at either side of it, to keep it private. He doesn't tell his parents that he's bought the house, but just says he's moving to the North of the country.

Within a month, he's organised for an interior decorator to furnish and decorate it. It is rather more contemporary than he would have chosen, with very little colour, but he doesn't anticipate living there for long periods of time and he had been happy to give the decorator a free rein.

It's a beautiful day. He's sat in his garden in Leeds, considering his next move, drinking an ice-cold beer and eating a hot roast beef sandwich, with a lot of horseradish, just the way he enjoyed eating it. He reminisces about his time at the art galleries with his gramps, talking to the stray cat that had come into the garden, probably enticed by the smell of the beef. He decides he needs to sort out the estate that he has been left.

The following day, he flies to Austria. He had spent the morning with the security firm that protected the artwork that he had inherited. During the conversation, the owner mentioned that he was considering retirement and was about to put the business up for sale.

Simon made a decision the very next morning and put a high offer on the table for the business, which was accepted straight away. He contacted his grandfather's solicitor, to get things moving.

He agreed with the owner that he would keep the original staff on, but wanted to advertise for a CEO to run the business on his behalf. As the business operated across Europe, he needed someone who was good with languages as well as finance and had excellent interpersonal skills.

He asks the HR department to set up an interview panel, with the intention of the new person being ready to start, as soon as the takeover was complete.

To relax, Simon spends a great deal of time looking at his grandfather's paintings and starts to think that he should complete his artwork idea in his gramps' memory.

After three gruelling weeks, they finally had their woman. Francis Jacobson, from France, who could speak several languages and was currently working for a successful finance company in Switzerland. She was ideal. She was to remain being based in Switzerland.

She would organise the recruitment of new staff or promote from the existing people, within the company, to develop her own new Management Team. Simon, being the owner, would have an office in Leeds, but he would leave the running of the business to Francis and only venture to the office for any really important video linked meetings or to sign anything that needed his approval.

Chapter Twelve

On the flight back to England, he makes a decision to alter his house in Leeds, so that he can start to experiment with the idea that he'd had whilst in Austria.

On one of the rare occasions, that he visits the Leeds office of his company, he checks the database to enquire about some of his employees on the books. He identifies a specialist builder, Phil Hogan, with the correct qualifications. He gets Phil on the phone and asks him to pay him a home visit.

When Phil arrives at the house, Simon shows him where he wants some alterations to his house. He informs him that he wants to create a large secret, soundproof, strong room, in case of a nuclear attack. He wants to add a bathroom with a bath, shower and toilet and an extra-large metal sink. He also needs refrigeration and enough room for a single bed, large table, chair and cabinet within the room.

He stipulates that he does the work 'off the books' and doesn't tell anyone else about the work. In return, he will offer him a substantial amount of money on completion of the job.

Phil thinks the man is completely bonkers and an eccentric but he's going to pay him well. At the end of the day, he's the owner of the company, so what the hell, if he wants an elaborate, very large and expensive bunker, then that's what he'll get. He's happy to keep it quiet. He doesn't want anyone else cashing in on any other potential work, that this guy might want doing in the future.

He can't wait to tell Sue about it when she gets back from her work conference and visiting her friend in Poland though. He rings her to tell her that he has had a windfall and has a surprise for her when she gets back. He thinks that if he times it right and works all the hours he can and gets a couple of other blokes to help out, he'll get this job finished by the time she gets back. He's going to get a good wedge of money from this, so offers to pay the two labourers, who don't work for the company, 'cash in hand', with his own money. He can't wait to see Sue. They'll have enough money to go on the holiday to Florida, that she wanted and a decent deposit to put on a house that she'd had her eye on. Maybe the trip to Florida could even be a honeymoon.

When Phil has eventually finished the work, he contacts his best friend, Micheal, to suggest a night out. He's been working all hours and tells him he's in need of a 'blow out'. Michael can't manage it, because he's not feeling well and the doctor has put him on antibiotics. Perhaps he would be feeling better the following week and they could go out into the City and let loose? Phil comes up with another idea that Michael is happier with.

On completion, after just two and a half weeks, Simon is stood admiring the work. Perfect for his purpose. He tells Phil, that he will put the money into his bank account the following day.

Now he needs to make sure that no one else knows about it. He follows Phil at 6pm, the day he's finished the work on his room. He takes the M62 out of Leeds. Simon follows at a safe distance in an old transit van that he bought, under a false name, the week before. It doesn't look like Phil is going home. He continues to follow him as he leaves the motorway towards the A58.

Phil stops at a Chinese takeaway, then proceeds to a house about a mile away. Simon waits until eleven-thirty that evening, for him to come out of the house he's been visiting and start the drive home. Simon had seen that a part of the road that they had driven down earlier had a steep embankment that went into a reservoir below. As they reach that part of the road, on their return, Simon swerved into Phil's car and watches as it turns over and rapidly rolls down into the water. Fortunately, because of the time, there's no other traffic on the road, so nobody sees the incident. Simon drives away. Later that day, he takes the transit van to the scrapyard and leaves it there.

The voices are mocking him. So you think you'll get away from us, do you? You're next! He racked his brain to see if he'd covered his tracks. Transit van bought in cash, from a private dealer, under a false name. Check... Dressed differently and used a different accent. Check... Wore gloves, so no fingerprints. Check. Wore overalls in the van, so no fibres left in the van. Check... He laughed at his voices, "There's no evidence back to me," he shouted, *even if they can trace the van back to the scrapyard*, he thought. With a bit of luck, it will be squashed beyond recognition by the time the police can trace it.

On Sue's return from her trip, she tries unsuccessfully to contact Phil. She doesn't get an answer on his mobile phone or at his apartment, so she contacts the police to express her concern for his safety. She tells them that he has had a windfall and had a surprise for her, so it would be out of character for him to just disappear.

The police discover that Phil had not used his debit or credit cards since the 3rd of October when he had used it to buy a takeaway. There was nothing unusual on his account. He wasn't overdrawn and there weren't any excessively large amounts either taken out or put into his account. It did appear that he'd drawn out, quite a bit more than he usually did, over the past couple of weeks.

Following further investigations, they discover that he had been to visit one of his friends, Michael, who confirmed that they had had a Chinese meal and a few drinks.

The police check the possible route he would have taken to get back home and discover that there are a few faint marks on the road that makes them think that a car could have driven off the road by the reservoir. It was difficult to see what could have caused the car to go off the road. It was a very busy road during the day. It was also notorious for cars driving too quickly. Nothing looked suspicious.

They organise for a diver to check the reservoir. They recover both the car and body from the water. On investigation, the car appeared to be in working order, before it had entered the reservoir. The Police concluded that the most likely event was that it was an accident.

They told her that his friend had said that Phil was tired, after working on a big job, although they didn't know what the job was, as no one could give them any information. The company he worked for, had told them that he had booked a few weeks off, so he hadn't been working on anything for them. He was probably driving a little too quickly, lost temporary control and due to the drink in his system, couldn't react quick enough to prevent the car from going over the edge. She was distraught that he'd died and angry that he'd been driving after drinking alcohol.

She contacted Micheal to see if he can shed any light on the job he had been working on, but he says that he never elaborated, apart from saying, he'd been on a good earner. They mostly talked about the football match that they had watched recently on TV. Phil had mentioned to him that he would be going on holiday soon though, but he had yet to organise it because it was supposed to have been a special surprise for her. Sue is left confused about his supposed windfall.

Chapter Thirteen

Simon, a few weeks after the demise of Phil and having heard nothing from the police, starts to venture out to the local opera house and the theatre, initially to shut out the noise of the voices in his head, but finds he is actually enjoying the diversions.

One Friday night, whilst having a drink in the interval of La Traviata, he meets Alice at the bar. He is initially attracted by the gold sparkly top that she's wearing. It reminds him of the painting, Judith by Klimt. During their conversation, she mentions that her mother is in a nursing home, suffering from dementia and she doesn't really get out very much, due to the time she spends visiting her mother. Simon asks her if she would like to go to the cinema with him. He believes that somewhere public would make him feel less conspicuous.

They arrange a date and time for him to pick her up from her house after they have decided which film to watch. She chooses the new Abba film, so even though it is not his preferred genre, he agrees that it will be a good one to go and see. He arranges to pick her up the following day. She is dressed casually, in a pair of black jeans and a pale blue sweater. They both agree that the film was much better than they had expected.

On the way out, he bumps into a man, with whom he went to school, with a woman, who he assumes to be his girlfriend or partner. "Hello Simon, long time no see." Simon instantly feels threatened. The voices are back, taunting him. After a quick "hello", he practically drags Alice out of the cinema, saying that his parking ticket will be running out soon and he doesn't want a fine.

"Who was that?"

"No one of interest," he spluttered. She decided not to pursue it, he is obviously feeling a bit shaken. Maybe he'll confide in her later. Simon can't believe that they have tracked him down. He knows that they are trying to sabotage his idea.

After the film, he drops her off at home and arranges another date, suggesting that he cooks her dinner at his place after she's been to see her mother. She asks him if he would like to go in for coffee, but he politely declines, saying that he has to be up early the following day. She rarely goes out, so this will be a real treat for her. She feels positively giddy at the thought of having a second date with such a lovely, caring and polite man.

When she visits her mother, the nurses complement her on how nice she looks. Alice has made a special effort for tonight's liaison and is pleased that others have noticed. She tells her mother that she is meeting a nice man for dinner. Her mother just smiles, not really comprehending anything she says to her.

He picks her up outside the gates of the nursing home, saying how lovely she looks. They go back to his house. Over a dinner of beef casserole, followed by chocolate fudge cake with cream that he'd bought at his local supermarket, he starts to ask her what she does, where she works, how she spends her leisure time and her friends.

He lies to her saying that he is a motor mechanic and was brought up in an orphanage.

He discovers that she works in a local bank, as an accountant. From their conversation, it didn't seem that she had any close friends and was a bit of a loner, probably because she said that she spent most of her free time visiting her mother. She did venture out to the cinema to watch a matinee occasionally but didn't appear to do much else. She was his perfect first candidate.

Since his return from Austria, he had carried out some extensive research on the Internet, identifying different types of paints that could be used on skin, to stop it from wrinkling. He also checked out other methods and processes that he would need to help him create his work. He had spent some time walking the streets at night, identifying drug users and watching them closely, to identify their dealers. It had taken a while, but he had finally managed to illegally purchase a batch of benzodiazepines midazolam and temazepam, to make up what was commonly known as the date drug from a drug dealer in Leeds. Now, he needed to start his experiment.

During dessert, he had drugged Alice's glass of wine. It wasn't long before the drug concoction, mixed with the alcohol, totally incapacitated Alice. Simon carries her through to his newly constructed room, undresses her and then slits her throat in the shower. He then proceeded to rinse himself down, dry off and put on his thermal clothing, before starting his first attempt at embalming. The temperature in the room is very cold.

He knows from his studies and his research on the Internet, that it takes a body between 24 to 72 hours to start breaking down and decomposing, and the internal organs to decompose from 3 to 5 days, but more importantly, the skin would turn blue after between 6 to 12 hours, so he needed to work quickly with his embalming process to preserve the skin and organs for as long as possible.

The skin already looked ashen, which was due to the lack of blood circulating in the body. He knew that when the blood settled in the body, the parts closest to the ground, would look bruised and turn a browny red colour, so he raised her head, to prevent the face from discolouring. He wanted something he could work with.

He has purchased the chemicals to embalm her, hoping to slow down the action of the cellular proteins, which in theory, he had read, would stop the cells acting as a nutrient for the bacteria within her body. This should then, kill the bacteria and slow down and maybe stop the purification process and give him the time to carry out his experimental work.

Although he believed he's completed the process well, after a couple of days, he had to insert a hollow needle into Alice's swollen body, to release the internal gasses that had formulated as bacteria within her. The smell is disgusting and he's glad that he is wearing a mask to repel the stench of rotting eggs.

Obviously, he hadn't quite managed to carry out the task of embalming as effectively as he had hoped. He makes a note to read up on the procedure again, to see where he went wrong. However, when surface mould starts to formulate on her feet, he knows that the decomposition has started to slow down.

He documents all the actions that he has taken and records what went well and areas that needed to be improved upon. He reads more on dissecting a body. He doesn't want to make any more mistakes. He then precedes to cut up Alice, to determine which parts would look best in his artwork. He takes time painting the skin. He uses the colours, gold, black, blue and red. He needs to see what effect this has on the texture of her skin. He then stores parts of the skin at different temperatures. He needs to check the effects over the next few months.

He puts the parts he's not using into the freezer, to stop them from decomposing, until he decides what to do with the remains.

After a further week of experiments, he visits a graveyard by the university, where he notices a funeral taking place. He spends some time watching the graveyard to monitor the activity during the week and at the weekend. He returns to the grave a couple of weeks later and buries her frozen remains in the same freshly dug resting place.

Afterwards, he disinfected his room and sits down to think of his next move. He switches on the television to watch the news, to see a picture of Alice, described as a missing person.

Thank goodness he has finished and effectively disposed off her body. After a few days from seeing the news, the police are knocking on his door, following up an enquiry that they had received from an old school friend of his, who had seen them both together at the cinema. Simon acted totally surprised to see them and said he hadn't seen the news.

He explained that they had been to the cinema once and had dinner, but when he asked her out again, she made an excuse that she was too occupied with her mother, to date again. He hadn't seen her since. He mentioned that over dinner, she had not seemed very happy about something, but he didn't like to pry, as they didn't really know each other well and he thought that maybe she just didn't like his company. She had told him that she was not enjoying her job but didn't say why. Before they left he said that he hoped that they would find her safe and well. Simon was angry with himself for not being more careful. He hoped that they would spend their time looking into the people that worked at her place of work, to give them some other potential suspects and keep them off his back.

The voices in his head were much more intimidating. They told him to beware, or he would be caught soon and taken to a place beyond even his comprehension. He decided that he would take his time before continuing his work, to ensure that he had covered all his tracks. He couldn't afford to make any mistakes this time. It was important to him, to finish what he'd started.

Chapter Fourteen

The next decision he had to make was the composition of his artwork. He spent nearly two months going through his collections, to determine the right works of art that he would work on.

He decided that the most prominent piece of his work would be a similarity to that of a sepia painting by Gustaf Klimt called Medicine, in honour of his gramps. He would use ideas from other artworks by the same artist for the rest of his idea and design them as one piece but display it three-dimensionally. He didn't want copies of the artist, but something more unique of his own choosing. He selected 'The Bride', which is an unfinished painting, the 'Faculty' paintings and lastly, 'The Death and Life'. Instead of creating a painting, he would create a cross between a painting and a sculpture and use a similar concept to the artworks that he'd chosen.

It had been six months since his experiment with Alice and the voices have been hounding him relentlessly. He decided to organise a flight and travel to Vienna to escape them. When he gets to the house in Vienna, he realises that hasn't eaten since the day before. Whilst he's out shopping for groceries, he sees a woman entering a high-class tailor's shop who catches his eye. She's quite plain but has a very clear complexion.

He enters the shop to discover that she is a shop assistant there. He asks her to show him some shirts that he needs for a function he has to attend for work. She asks him what style and colour he would like to look at. He laughs saying that he has no idea. He says that he doesn't really understand fashion and he would happily rely on her judgement, as long as it's not multi-coloured or covered in pineapples. He tells her a tale about how he turned up at a function in odd shoes once because he just picks up the nearest thing when he's getting dressed. He says that they all had a good laugh about it.

He buys two new shirts and a pair of trousers and a contrasting jacket then heads off to the deli for the rest of his groceries and grabs a pastry to eat on his way back to the house to take away the hunger pain in his stomach.

The following week, he goes back into the tailor's on the pretext of buying a new suit. He makes sure he is served by the same shop assistant. She remembers him from the week before. She is very attentive and chatty. He informs her that everyone had commented on his attire at his function and it was all down to her good taste. She is flattered when he asks her if she would like to have lunch with him. He introduces himself as John Franks.

"I'm Melissa James," she replied. He finds out that she lives alone and doesn't have any family. She says that she has a couple of close friends, Jennifer and Holly.

He escorts her back to the shop, and they arrange to meet for a drink the following day. They are getting on famously. He makes her laugh. She suggests another get together and says she would like him to meet her friends. He agrees that it would be a great idea but an hour before they are due to get together, he rings to say that his car has been in a minor accident, but not to worry but he has to cancel. He arranges to meet her another time to take her out to dinner, just the two of them. He makes sure that they never have the chance to meet up with her friends. When she comes up with a date that they can all get together, he tells her he has a prior arrangement. Eventually, she stops trying to get them together. He laughs about it, saying that they are obviously never meant to meet.

He rents an apartment in the name of David Jinks, where they spend a lot of time together, eating dinner or watching a movie, but rarely venture out anywhere public, apart from going out for the occasional walk and never to the same place, or going for a drive, out into the countryside. They occasionally go out for dinner, but again, never to the same place.

After dinner at a new restaurant in the town, she invites him back to her house. He agrees to stay the night. Whilst having a drink, he picks up a photograph album from a bookcase. She goes through the snaps, showing him pictures of herself and her two friends on holiday and relates funny stories that took place, at the time, when the pictures were taken.

He believes someone is trying to persecute him and is paranoid that he is being watched, so waits for her to go to sleep, then searches through her desk to look for any evidence that she might be spying on him. He comes across her passport, takes down the details and returns it. He looks through her phone, to make sure that she hasn't taken a photograph of him. He continues to search through her house until he's satisfied that there is nothing to find that can do him any harm. He then ventures back to bed. She is still fast asleep and oblivious of him searching through her belongings.

After they have been seeing each other for a month, he tells her, that as a surprise, he has organised a trip for her birthday. All he would tell her was that it was somewhere local and a secret, although he intimated, after, not a lot of persuasion that it might be to a place with a jacuzzi and specialists providing body treatments. She is over the moon. She had never been treated to such a lovely present before. She had been to a spa with Holly and Jennifer a few months ago and thoroughly enjoyed the experience. She can't wait to tell her friend, Holly that he is taking her to a spa, for her birthday. On her birthday, she is even more surprised to find out that they are flying to their destination.

When they set off to the airport, he says that she just needs to relax and enjoy her birthday. He says he wants to spoil her and that he will take care of everything that needs to be done and hopes that she is not disappointed that they weren't going to the spa after all. He booked the internal flights in false names, but she is totally unaware of this. She's all smiles, whilst drinking her glass of champagne. They fly to Salzburg and then he hires a car and drives on the A1 towards one of the houses he inherited from his grandfather. The house is near Lake Attersee, is very secluded and has beautiful views. She is thrilled. It is so romantic.

That evening, whilst drinking a good bottle of claret, from his grandfather's collection, Melissa starts to feel a little woozy. The last thing she sees is Simon smiling down at her. He wants the skin on her face, so decides to stab her with a very sharp kitchen knife, in the heart. He then proceeds to carefully start peeling away the skin from her face, stretches it, paints it, then puts it in the cold cellar to dry. The following day, he disinfects the kitchen, cleans up and checks his work. The voices resurface, saying that he can't get rid of them that easily. That night, when all is quiet, he takes the body, wrapped in sacking and weighted down with metal chains, to the middle of the lake, using a small motorboat that is at the side of the house and disposes of her.

Before he flies back to England, he buys the appropriate equipment, needed for his work and sets up an art studio, in the house by the lake, with all the materials he will need for his final masterpiece. He then returns to Vienna to thoroughly clean Melissa's home, in an effort to remove any evidence of his presence.

A week later, he flies back to Heathrow in London, then catches a flight to Manchester. From there, he travels back to Leeds via train. He then organises the exportation of some of the things that he will need whilst visiting Austria. He knows that he can't stay long in the same place, or the voices will catch up with him.

Meanwhile, in Vienna, the police place Melissa on the report as a missing person. They do not have any obvious leads to her whereabouts. They try to locate John Franks, but this is a dead-end.

He doesn't appear to exist. When the police search her property for clues, they notice that her passport is in the drawer, so she's not gone abroad. There is no forensic evidence either. However, they believe, from her friends, that she must be somewhere local and spend their time searching the local area and spas.

Her friends tell the Police that they know that he had an apartment in the middle of town and give them the address that Melissa had mentioned to them. When they investigate, they discovered that he didn't live there, but couldn't locate the actual occupier either. They had no leads. The apartment had been thoroughly cleaned, by professional contract cleaners that Mr Jinks had arranged and paid for in cash. The rooms smelt of bleach. There were no fingerprints either. It was as though no one had ever lived there. Neither men appear to exist. The Police escalated their missing person file, to an unsolved murder, even though they have no body.

Chapter Fifteen

Simon received an unexpected call from Dawn on his third night back in Leeds. When he answers, she says that she was staying in Leeds, visiting a friend and thought she'd call him to see if he wanted to go out for dinner, for old times' sake. He wasn't planning anything for that evening and he was curious to know what she wanted, so agreed to meet her in the City. She noticed that he didn't offer to pick her up and he sounded much more confident from when she had last met him, if not a bit formal.

She had made an effort to wear an outfit that he had bought her, but it was obvious to her, that it hadn't registered with him. He was a totally different person, to the one that she could so easily manipulate before. After dinner, he didn't try to arrange another get-together, or even offer her a lift back to her friend's. She realised that there was no point in trying. Even with all her wiles, she wasn't going to be able to hook him. He had been quite cold with her and she knew, instinctively, that he wasn't interested in renewing their relationship.

After they had finished their meal, she suggested they went on to a club, but he said he had other things that he needed to attend to that evening and set off walking down the road towards the taxi rank. He didn't even say goodnight. She watched him get into a cab. He didn't look back, or acknowledge her, as he drove past, a few moments later. He just looked through her, as if she didn't exist. The realisation, that there was nothing she could do to change the situation, deflated her.

Even though it was late, she went straight to the train station and bought a ticket back to London. After all, she didn't know anyone, other than Simon, in Leeds. Her train didn't go for another hour and a half, so she sat drinking a coffee on the platform, while thinking how stupid she had been for not staying with him. She had lost all the things that she coveted, like a fancy house and expensive sparkly jewellery. She'd find it hard to find another meal ticket as good as that one.

When Simon returned home, he felt relieved. The voices had warned him about her, but it looked like he was safe from her, but to be sure, he needed to leave for Austria as soon as possible.

Before he returns, he has some business to conclude with his company. He tells Francis that, although the firm's doing exceptionally well, he has decided to sell. She says that she is really sorry to hear that because she had some great ideas to expand the business that she would have liked to have run by him. He then asks her if she would be interested in purchasing it. He offers it to her, well below market value, to be paid in manageable instalments, so that she can afford to buy it.

Francis can't believe her luck. He tells her that he has plenty of money and doesn't have the inclination to expand. Over the next couple of weeks, he gets his solicitor to draw up the paperwork and once it's complete, throws a party, in

London for all his employees. At the party, he acknowledges everyone's hard work and announces the new ownership. He has paid for his employees to travel from their various locations in Europe and for their lodgings. They are all amazed at his generosity. This would be the first and last time, that some of them, had seen him, or come into contact with him. He came across to them all as an extremely pleasant man without any airs and graces.

He is feeling unusually elated. He has successfully carried out his experiments and is moving forwards with his masterpiece. He has lots of ideas formulating in his head and the voices trying to impede him, can't catch him. He had managed to get rid of his security company and now has no association with it, to distract him from his real passion. Even the voices were subdued.

He spends his time, travelling to visit Jessy and her husband, making sure that they have everything that they need. He goes out to the cinema and opera and even considers buying a dog, after watching a movie on television. When he's satisfied that all is well, he decides that getting a dog isn't such a good idea and would be more of a hindrance than a pleasurable companion and it would scupper his plans for the future. Now that everything is running smoothly, Simon decides that he would fly back to Austria.

Chapter Sixteen

On the evening of his return to Vienna, he goes to the theatre. In the foyer is the most beautiful looking woman he has ever seen. Her name is Catherine Fitzpatrick, a fashion model. She is perfect for his artwork. From a distance, she looks like she has good skin, but he especially likes her eyes. They seem to smile when she talks.

When he returns home, he fires up his computer and logs onto the different search engines. He searches for her and finds out when and where she is going to be, over the next few weeks. He knows that there is no chance of her being interested in him, so he makes a point of following her as discreetly as possible. Luckily, she doesn't appear to notice him and is usually surrounded by her entourage. The voices tell him that she will be a challenge. This makes him even more determined. He is not going to let them sabotage his work again.

He continues to follow her over the next couple of weeks. She takes a flight to France for a photo shoot. Simon has been watching her closely. She seems to lead a mad frenzied existence. She works and plays hard, walking down catwalks or being photographed during the daytime and partying in the evening. She is continually busy, but puts some time aside to be alone, every day. He obviously can't get access to everywhere she goes but makes every effort to be as close as possible to her, without causing any suspicion. He doesn't want to be accused of stalking her.

She's admired everywhere she goes, but doesn't appear to be phased by all the fuss and is happy to sign autographs. He believes that she must be tired. She hardly eats and she's stick thin. She reminds him, a lot, of his mother. She always looks immaculate. Her clothes are expensive-looking and she is always made up to the nines. He concludes that being a well-known model, probably means that she gets all her clothes and cosmetics for free. This thought reminded him of a song by a singer, whose name he couldn't recall at the moment. She was a walking, talking, living doll, advertising billboard. He wonders what her skin must be like under all that plaster on her face.

Her flight returns to Austria at eight in the morning. When they land, she tells everyone that she wants to be alone for a while, to recoup her energy and she'll call her agent later that afternoon. She catches a taxi from the airport, back to her apartment. Simon knows where she lives and follows her in his car that he had left at the airport. She goes to her apartment, puts on her jogging pants and a baggy tee-shirt and makes herself a cup of green tea.

At around 10am, the doorbell rings. There's a man in overalls at her door with a parcel. She opens the door and before she realises it, the man has put a cloth over her nose and she passes out. Simon drags her back into the apartment, gauges out her eyes and puts them into the fluid that he has brought with him. He then cuts off her left hand. He puts his precious cargo into a specialist container, to keep them as fresh as possible. He takes off his uniform which is covered in blood and puts it into a plastic bag, then shuts the door and leaves, putting his gloves into his pocket. Once in his car, he puts his body parts into his suitcase.

He had previously organised the hire of a private plane back to Salzburg, so he drives back to the airport. He leaves his car in the long-stay car park and boards his internal flight, after stopping at the restrooms to check his appearance. When he arrives in Salzburg, he drives back to his house by the lake. He carries out his preparations for his work of art, then puts it into storage.

Catherine's agent tries to contact her later that day, as she hadn't been in touch. It was so unlike her and they had been invited to dinner that evening with the editor of the most prestigious magazine in London. He really needed to talk with her before they met, so he could negotiate a deal that would be beneficial to both of them.

When he gets no reply, he drives round to her place but doesn't get an answer. He tries the door, only to discover that it's unlocked. When he enters, he vomits at the sight of her lying on the floor, with two gaping holes in her face, where her eyes used to be, obviously dead. He rings the police and asked them to keep it as low key as possible. He doesn't want the media to know about the murder yet until he can process it and sort out any potential contractual issues.

He's in shock and can't think straight.

When the chief investigator arrives, he immediately clears the area and calls for a forensic team. They cannot find any evidence, but the team soon realises that there are potentially many possible suspects. Because of the media response this would generate, they would have to be very thorough, which would mean it was going to take a long time and stretch their resources.

Simon spends another month at the lake house until the voices start interrupting his thoughts. He is taking time to relax. He feels exhausted after watching Catherine working.

Whilst drinking a gin and tonic on his balcony, watching the sun go down, he was thinking that he had made the correct decision about not using her skin. It wasn't in good condition. The hand was a bonus. He hadn't intended to take it until the very last minute but was so pleased that he had. It had made a big difference to his piece. During the night, whilst tossing and turning in bed, the voices told him that they knew where he was. He gets out of bed and packs a suitcase, in preparation, to fly back to England the following day.

Chapter Seventeen

When he lands at Manchester, his bags are nowhere to be seen. He's not the only person to be waiting for their bags. A woman, who is obviously annoyed, asks him if this had ever happened to him before. He says that it happens quite regularly and not to be concerned. He's always had it delivered to his address later if they can't find it straight away. It will probably still be in Vienna.

They start to talk. Her name is Vivienne Spinks, a property developer from Manchester. They go for a coffee together at the arrivals lounge and wait to hear where their suitcases are. She tells him that she's married with a son, who is six years of age. It's obvious to Simon that she is not happily married, as she says that because of her work, she and her husband don't get much time to spend together and when they do, they tend to spend their time arguing. He discovers that she is managing a new development at a resort, nearby his house by the lake.

She tells him that she travels back to see her family as regularly as possible. Although she loves her son dearly, she says it's a strain on her and it would be better if she stayed nearer the development on a more frequent basis, mainly because it was costing such a lot of her own money and it would be much more convenient and quicker if she was more available on site. She says that the quicker she finishes the contract, the sooner she would be able to spend quality time with her family.

She tells him that she doesn't know anyone in Austria, apart from the people working on the plans and says she doesn't like staying in a hotel on her own, as it's a lonely existence. He suggests that she stays with him when she's next over, on a purely platonic basis, of course.

They are getting on well and he seems like a gentleman. She says she will contact him when she's flying over next. He gives her one of his mobile telephone numbers but doesn't expect her to contact him. After nearly two hours of drinking coffee and eating at the cafe whilst waiting to hear something about their cases, they leave to go their separate ways home. His suitcase arrives at his door, in Leeds, the following day.

He spends some time, checking out his rough plans for his artwork so that he can plan which body part he needs to collect next. He notices that he has a missed call on his landline from his father. He presses the answer button to hear the message. "Hello, Simon. It's your father, I am calling to see if you are okay. We haven't heard from you for a while. Speak with you soon. Goodbye."

Simon laughed. "So they are trying to track me down, are they?" He telephoned back.

His mother answered, "Hello."

"Mother, its Simon. I understand that father wanted to check that I was okay. Just to let you know that I'm well and in Scotland on holiday."

"Ah good, well look after yourself and I'll let your father know when he gets back from work."

"Goodbye mother."

"Goodbye Simon." Short and sweet. Now he's put them off his trail. He was surprised that she had never asked him where he was living, but that it was possibly because someone else had already told her.

A week later, he receives a text from Vivienne to let him know that she is flying to Vienna the day after and would it be okay if she stayed at his place. He immediately rang the airport to book a flight, then texted her back saying that he looked forward to seeing her again and by coincidence, he had to go back for business on the same day. At the airport lounge, they meet up and he says he will come and pick her up from the site when she finishes work. They board the flight and chat about her stay at home and her project in Austria, until they arrive at their destination.

She contacted him at about 6pm. He picked her up and then drove back to his house. He showed her his spare room, so she could get settled, before dinner, that he had prepared earlier. She was staying for three days then flying back home. The following couple of days, he taxied her back to the site and then back to his. He told her she could stay again on her return. "Please, just let me know when you'll be back, so I can tidy up." She had really enjoyed being there. It was peaceful and she had been able to relax for the first time in ages. He had been true to his word and had been a gentleman the whole time that she had been there, so she trusted him inexplicably.

She had told her husband and work colleagues that she was staying at a hotel. Even though it was a perfectly respectable setup with Simon, she didn't want them to get the wrong impression of her. He had laughed when she told him. "All very hush-hush then. I quite like the secrecy." They both flew back to Manchester. Simon offers her a lift home, but she declines. She had already organised for a taxi to pick her up. He suggests that they go out for dinner one night to discuss some plans that he has for some renovations on his house in Austria.

On her return home, she discovers that Shaun, her husband, has arranged a visit to his mother's for a long weekend. She tells him that she can't go, as she has too much paperwork to complete, before her trip back to Austria and she would prefer it, if they waited until her job was finished, before organising trips off. He accuses her of putting work before them, which leads to an almighty row, where she tells him to go without her.

When Shaun and Josh, her son, leave, Vivienne is annoyed that he couldn't have been more accommodating. She reasoned, that their relationship was just going through a bad patch and it would be so much better, once she had the job finished in Austria. She would miss seeing Josh though. If she had known, they'd be having an argument on her return, she would have stayed put.

She rang Simon to say that she was free that evening to discuss the renovations since her husband had abandoned her. She told him that her husband and son were going to her husband's mother's for a few days, so they could meet up after she had completed some of her work, later that evening.

Simon suggests that Shaun would probably phone her later to apologise. Maybe she should ring him to say where she was going, in case he started to worry when he couldn't get an answer. She explains that her husband would misinterpret their relationship, if she told him about their meeting and that, from previous experience, it would be most unlikely that he would contact her until tomorrow when he would have had time to cool down after their row.

He arranged to pick her up at seven that evening. When he arrived, she was at the door, in her coat, ready to go. He drove her to his house in Leeds. However, during dinner, she starts to feel uneasy. Simon's demeanour had changed. It was as though he wasn't really listening to what she was saying.

During the main course, she started to feel disconnected. Simon came over to her and watched as she fell asleep, never to wake up again. He had successfully poisoned her. He prepared the parts he wanted from her and felt quite pleased with himself, but his feelings were tinged with sadness. He had genuinely liked her.

He drives to the graveyard again, to see if he could find any grave that he could utilise that would be easy to dig through. He managed to find a grave belonging to an elderly man that would be ideal for his purpose. That night, he went to the graveyard and carried out the task of disposing of Vivienne's remains. He smiled to himself.

They hadn't managed to track him down. He had them all fooled.

As expected, Shaun tried to phone Vivienne at home the following day after their argument, but he wasn't getting a response. She was obviously upset with him, but it wasn't usual for her to ignore his calls, in case he needed to talk to her about Josh. He decided to cut his visit short. He made a decision to leave Josh with his grandparents, while he sorted things out with Vivienne. When he arrived home and she wasn't there, he became concerned. She wasn't answering her mobile phone either.

He reported her missing to the police, but couldn't tell them anything, apart from the disagreement that they'd had the previous day and that it looked like she had finished some work that she had been doing when he left. There was no obvious sign of a break-in or a struggle.

The police questioned Shaun under caution, for over two hours about his relationship with his wife, but it was obvious that he hadn't hurt his wife and he had a firm alibi from his parents. That didn't mean that he couldn't have arranged her disappearance though and they had to look at every angle. They mounted a search, but it didn't look promising that they would find her, based on the information they had.

They contacted her employer, to find out if she had been in any kind of trouble, or if she had any problems with staff etc. One of the directors contacted the Police a few days later, saying that they had spoken to the guys on-site, but they had said that she kept herself to herself and they hadn't seen anything out of the ordinary. A detective flew over to question the men on site personally but didn't get any further information. It appeared that they kept themselves to themselves and didn't socialise with each other out of work.

Chapter Eighteen

Simon's telephone has been ringing for quite some time. He answers to find his father on the line. "Simon, we have been worried about you, when are you coming down to London to see us?" He is very wary. They have never expressed concern about him before and certainly never invited him to visit. He was curious.

"I'll come to you in a couple of days' time if that's okay?"

"We'll look forward to it."

"See you then."

"Amelia, Simon is coming to visit in a couple of days' time. It might be a good idea if you were around too. I'd like to know just what my father left him and what Simon intends to do with his money. We could suggest that he invest in my business. We've been so busy lately that I would like to expand."

"It's only right that he does, Edward. After all, he was, 'your' father."

The only reason Edward wanted his son's money was because Amelia had been spending a ridiculous amount of money lately. The new, shiny bright yellow sports car she'd purchased, had cost an arm and a leg. He wouldn't have minded but she hadn't even driven it yet. It had been sat in one of the garages for a fortnight. Then only last week, she'd flown to Dubai with a girlfriend, from the golf club and come back with an armful of gold bangles and god only knows, what else.

He could have afforded to fund the expansion that he wanted, but reasoned that he'd rather spend his money on more exciting things, such as the holiday that they had booked to go to Fiji next month. They were going to view a few properties, whilst they were there. He'd heard that you could get a really good property for a very reasonable price since the Tsunami had struck the island. For once, he thought, Amelia was right about him being eligible for some of Maxwell's money. It wouldn't harm anyone to take a little of the money from Simon.

When Simon arrives, he is surprised that they have had dishes prepared that, in his younger days, would not have been allowed. This heightens his suspicion. After dinner, which he hardly touches, just in case they are trying to poison him, he goes out to a local well-known nightclub, thinking that it would be hard for them to track him there. The music is so loud, he can feel the floor vibrating. There are coloured strobe lights moving around the dance floor, mesmerising him and making his eyes hurt. He moves away from the cacophony and heads to the bar for a drink.

At the bar, he meets a woman called Lorraine Senior. She tells him that she is a newspaper reporter. He tells her who he is and who his parents are. They go upstairs and find a side table, well away from the noise, to talk. She is very interested and wants to know more about his family. He says that he will unlock all the family secrets, but not tonight. Tonight, he just wants a few drinks and to relax.

They arrange to meet at the end of the week at his father's place because he knows that they are flying out to Switzerland. He gives her his telephone number and the address of his parents' house. He tells her to ring him first, to make sure that his parents have not changed their minds and stayed in London. She agrees. Although she'd like to meet them, she knows he won't be able to give her a story if they are there.

When he returns back to his parents', they quiz him to find out where he's been. He says that he has been for a walk and called at a public house that was serving after hours, for a drink. He said he couldn't remember the name of the pub, but it was a bit seedy.

The following morning, at breakfast, he feels like he is being interrogated. His mother wanted to know where he was living and how he was spending his time. This only served to heighten his cautiousness. He answered very economically. "I'm living in the North and my work involves a lot of travel."

"Yes dear, but what kind of work are you doing?"

"Nothing of interest. It's to do with health and safety. Tell me about what you've been up to mother."

Amelia spent the next half an hour telling him about her trip to Dubai and her new car.

Finally, after determining that he wasn't going to disclose any further information about himself, and the obvious lack of interest he was showing in what Amelia had been prattling on about, Edward asked him about his inheritance. He answered that he had enough to live on. Edward went into great detail, about how he wanted to expand his business, but could do with an injection of funds and asks Simon if he would like to invest. Amelia interjected to say that he would get it all back someday with interest when they died.

He hasn't really been listening, but he's got the gist of what his father wants from him. Simon told him that if he wanted Maxwell's vineyard, he could have it, as long as he dealt with the sale etc. His father went into the kitchen and instantly called his broker to find out how much it was worth. He is pleasantly surprised that it will easily fund his venture and he'll have some money left over for any little extras. When he returns to the dining room he gets Simon to telephone his solicitor straight away. "We need to strike while the iron's hot," says his father. Now Simon knows why his parents asked him to visit, he feels less worried for his safety. They are certainly not going to harm him, at least, until the sale goes through.

Chapter Nineteen

Lorraine is ecstatic. She is finally going to get her scoop. She'll show the editor at the paper that she can make the grade. Arty had been on her back, about writing something worth printing, for the past six months, since she started.

She had made a mistake early on, by discussing with Kevin, another new recruit, an idea that she had about a local footballer that she was going to investigate and write about. Kevin had talked to Arty about it. She couldn't believe her ears when it was announced that Kevin had come up with an idea that the paper was going to run with. Following this, Kevin became the blue-eyed boy. She wouldn't make that mistake again. She wasn't going to tell anyone about her meeting with Simon Harrington.

That weekend, she promptly shows up at his father's house. She is full of enthusiasm about her first big story. Simon has prepared everything in advance of her arrival. He's organised the drug mixture and the instruments that he needs. He offers her a drink. She asks for a coffee while admiring his father's house. She gets straight into the interview. Lorraine is eager to know as much as possible.

He asks her what she has said to her Editor at the paper. Lorraine tells him that he doesn't even know that she's there, nor does anyone else for that matter. She has kept their meeting strictly confidential as she wants the interview to be exclusive to herself. Little does she know that she has just signed her own death warrant.

She switches on her recorder and starts to ask him basic questions about his upbringing. After half an hour, he pours two large glasses of red wine and offers her one. She says she doesn't want one, but Simon insists that it's a special bottle of wine that he opened twenty minutes ago, to allow it to breathe, and he doesn't want it to go to waste. She's intrigued by the effort he appears to have gone to, so a little reluctantly, she takes the glass from him. She doesn't normally drink when she's following up on an assignment.

He starts to feel very frustrated. She isn't drinking the wine as quickly as he wants her to. He encourages her to drink, by offering her a top-up. She sips some more. "What do you think of the wine?" he asks. She takes another sip.

"It's very nice, thank you. I don't normally drink good wine, so it's probably wasted on me. You could have opened a cheap bottle of plonk and I wouldn't have noticed any difference."

He starts to answer her questions about his family, while she continues to drink her wine. At last, her speech starts to slow down and she sits there staring at him. He steers her into his car and starts driving to Leeds. Halfway there, he pours more of the drugged drink down her throat, so that she will be easy to manipulate when he gets her back to his house.

When they get back, he parks his car in the drive and then walks her inside the house. He takes her into his secret room and undresses her. He puts her clothes into a disposal bag, washes his hands and decides to cut out the body parts that he wants without stabbing or poisoning her. For the short time that she's alive, she screams silently in agony. Later that evening, he takes her remains to the graveyard and disposes of her.

Early the next morning, he sets off on his drive back to London. He stops at the service station for a bite to eat, then continues on his travels. He arrives at his father's house, takes a shower, changes his clothes, puts his belongings into his car and then drives to the airport to pick up his parents. Once he has dropped them off, he drives all the way back to Leeds. By the time he gets back, he is shattered. He has a splitting headache and the voices are back with a vengeance.

Because reporters, whilst 'following up a story', sometimes, go 'off the radar', no one missed her until two weeks later. The police were brought in, but there were no clues as to her whereabouts. She was last seen in a nightclub, that she frequented regularly, talking to someone a fortnight earlier, but nobody could describe him, as it had been a busy night and no one took any real notice. She was filed as a missing person, but Arty said that she was probably chasing up a story and she would turn up sooner or later. However, after a month, he contacted the police to inform them, that she had not been in touch.

After a couple of weeks, Simon flew back to Austria to escape the voices and decided to collect his other art pieces, to bring back to Leeds, so that he could, at last, start to construct his artwork properly. On his way to the house, he stopped by the lake to watch the water and talk to his gramps, to tell him about the voices and the conspiracy.

He very nearly had all his components. He was concerned about getting through customs, on his way home, but thought he had disguised his wares well. He had spent time, adapting his large suitcase, so that the parts that he had preserved were well disguised and was hoping that if he was stopped and questioned, he could convince them that they weren't real, but very good imitations for a television film he was working on. This was the riskiest part of the journey so far. His canvasses were being flown separately, with some more mundane pieces that he had picked up from a local art exhibition.

He had taken a flight at a time that he knew would be busy. He was extremely lucky when he was going through customs at Heathrow. He had planted drugs on a man at the airport in Austria, who had appeared to have managed to get on the plane undetected. However, when they landed, he was stopped at customs. They checked his briefcase, found the drugs and went to detain him. He panicked and tried to make a dash for it. The security staff chased after him and brought him down to the ground. In all the melee, Simon sauntered through, without being checked and stopped. He went to the Avis desk and hired a car, for his drive back to Leeds and breathed a sigh of relief.

Chapter Twenty

On his return, he is invited to one of his father's parties. He decides to travel down for the weekend. He is interested to see what they want from him now. All the way there, he is arguing with the voices in his head. By the time he arrives, he's exhausted. He feigns a migraine and goes to bed.

After a couple of hours, Lydia brings him some food and a hot drink and leaves a couple of pills by his bedside. He is awake and has been since he came up to his room. He eats the snack and downs the coffee but puts the pills in the bedside cabinet. He is starting to settle down again and picks up a novel to read, that had been left on the bedside table. After ten minutes, he puts down the book, gets dressed and goes out for a walk.

He arrives back with an hour to spare before the party is due to start. He genuinely has no idea where he has been but he is feeling cold. He takes a hot shower, to warm up his body, gets dressed and goes downstairs. He is greeted by all the usual colour and glamour that can be found at his parent's parties.

At the party, he is introduced to Louise Clement, one of the many socialites, who his parents had decided, would be a good match for him. Simon shows her no interest, thinking that it was some form of an elaborate ploy by his parents to entrap him, take his money and have him killed. Louise has never been ignored in this way before and is more determined than ever to pursue him. During the evening, she even follows him through to the kitchen when he goes to get a drink of water. She talks about the people that she knows well in the entertainment business, in an effort to try to impress him, but all her chatter falls on deaf ears. She can see that he isn't interested in what she is saying, but carries on, hoping that he will eventually engage in conversation with her, even if it is just to shut her up. Her voice is starting to grate on his nerves. Simon doesn't offer an excuse to leave the party and just goes up to his room, midway through her conversation, ignoring the perplexed look on her face. Out of habit, he automatically locks the door.

Not long after he has gone up to his room, he hears and sees the handle trying to turn. Louise is whispering through the door. "Simon, it's me. Let me in. I thought I could cheer you up." He chooses to ignore her. She tries again, "Simon, its Louise. Let me in." She surmises, that like her, when she's at home in bed, he must have put on his headphones to listen to music and he couldn't hear her. Eventually, he hears her moving away from his door and he can hear her footsteps walking towards the top of the staircase.

She reminds him of his mother. She is as thin as a rake, heavily made-up and glides around the room like a praying mantis. When he gets up, the morning after, he discovers that she has been invited to lunch by his parents. Over lunch, he tells them all that he has a girlfriend in Leeds called Angela, in an effort to put them off the scent, because he doesn't trust them and believes that they are manoeuvring to kill him. He notices the surprise on his mother's face. He's not sure if she's surprised that he has a girlfriend, or that he has disclosed that he is living in Leeds. The voices told him that she probably thinks he's still seeing Dawn and that she already knows where he's living.

Louise mentions to her friends that probably the most eligible bachelor was seeing someone. They tell her that if he's not married then he's still available and even if he was married, he was still worth the effort. "Think of everything you could do with his kind of money," said her closest friend, Maria. Louise decides to travels to Leeds, on the pretence that she needs to talk with him urgently about his parents. She says that she needs to speak with him face to face. She knew from previous experience that he would put her off from travelling to see him, if she couldn't come up with a good excuse. When he gets the call from her, he's surprised. After all, he thought he had made it quite clear that he wasn't interested. Although he's suspicious, he gives her his address and they arrange a time and date for her visit. However, when she gets there, she admits that it was a lie so that she could see him again.

She did not want to be humiliated, so she hasn't mentioned to Maria that she was going to see him. She knows that she would be the talk of the whole city if he brushed her aside, and she didn't want anyone to think she was a gold digger or even worse, desperate.

However, she was only there because the thought of his money was an aphrodisiac.

After she had told him that it was a ploy of hers to see him on his own, he decided that it was better if they stayed in, rather than go out for dinner. He felt safer in his own house. Louise made a lot of effort to entice him into having a relationship with her. She flirted outrageously. He engages her in conversation about her close friends, to ascertain who knew she was there. He's happy with her answers. He decided that he may as well make use of her since she was so obviously eager. She wasn't clever enough to be a threat to him. She asked to use his bathroom after dinner. She changed her clothes and dressed in something more alluring that she thought would appeal to him. They ended up in bed together. He didn't enjoy the intimacy and she left him cold. It was just a function that he had to go through but he wasn't attracted to her and for all her best efforts he couldn't get excited or an erection. She reminded him too much of his mother. She felt as though she had failed. This had never happened to her before. Usually, men couldn't wait to get her into bed. How can he not be attracted to her? She felt cheap. It was too late to go home and she was too embarrassed to leave, so she laid in his bed, with her back to him, until she eventually fell to sleep.

He lay awake for much of the night, not totally sure if she was going to harm him. His paranoia had started to escalate during the night. He was convinced that she was waiting for him to go to sleep and then she'll suffocate him. The voices had warned him. He had regretted telling her where he lived. He had taken a risk when he was usually so careful. He realised that he has been lax and he would have to be much more careful in the future.

He strangled her the next morning while she slept. He checked her phone, to see if she had mentioned her visit to him. Finding that she hadn't, he smashed it. There had been nothing on her phone about her trip to see him. She had kept his address on a piece of paper in her handbag, so it appeared, that she had told him the truth the previous evening and no one knew she was there. He took her body into his safe room, dismembered her and cleaned up. He had become quite proficient at dissection and was pleased with his own, self-taught, skills. He sliced off both her breasts. He disposed of the unused remains at his usual place in the graveyard later that night. He felt nothing for her, but distain.

There's an investigation in London to find her after her friend Maria reports that she hasn't seen or heard from her in a while. The police investigate, but they cannot track her whereabouts. Her last call was made from her London flat to Simon Harrington in Leeds, but she hadn't used her phone since. They questioned Simon's parents and discovered that he met her at their house at a party, but he hadn't really shown any interest in her and as far as they knew, they certainly hadn't arranged to see each other again. This was collaborated by others who had attended the party. It was obvious that she was a very popular young woman, who was never short of a partner.

They asked the branch in West Yorkshire to question him, but he substantiates what his parents have said. He adds that they had lunch at his parents' house and she had phoned to ask him to find out when he would next be in London. He tells the policewoman that he didn't really know her but he had told her he would contact her when he went back to his parents and they could grab a coffee. The police officer reported back that he was plausible and she did not suspect him of any crime. The police in London think that she could have been murdered in London, but without any leads and no evidence, they have to leave the case open.

Chapter Twenty-One

Simon was driving down the motorway at seventy miles an hour, listening to Beethoven's Fifth Symphony, when the voices started to invade his thoughts again. He turned up the volume in an effort to clear them from his mind. He saw a sign up ahead, indicating that he was approaching a service station. He slowed down as he was nearing the exit so that he could get off the motorway and buy a coffee.

He parked the car and walked inside the building to the cafeteria. He paid for his coffee and sat down at a table nearest the window. On the adjacent table, sat a woman sipping her coffee, whilst reading through some paperwork and making notes. She looked up to see him watching her. She smiled and he reciprocated.

When she'd finished, she packed up her things and walked away from the table. At the same time, he got up from his chair as she was passing his table and deliberately bumped into her. The papers that she was carrying fell onto the floor.

"I can't apologise enough. I'm so sorry. I didn't see you."

"Please don't worry about it, they are only rough notes for a lecture that I'm giving in Manchester."

He helped her pick up the sheets of paper and noticed that they were notes about different films. "So, you are interested in film?" he asked.

"Yes," she replied. "I'm at the University tomorrow, to discuss filmmaking."

"Well, good luck. Hope it goes well." He says as they both leave for their cars.

When he gets to his car, he contacts the University to find out more about the lecture and discovers that it starts at 2pm tomorrow and will be given by Taneal Clayton. He then looks up her name on the internet, to see what he can find out about her.

The following day, he parks his hired car near the University car park and watches as she arrives at the University at one fifteen. She's driving the same car that she was driving yesterday. He reads a book until she reappears at the car park exit, then follows her home. He waits outside to watch. No one else enters or leaves her house.

He's still there in the morning when she drives away.

He goes home to freshen up and have a bite to eat. Later that day, he returns to her house and notices that her car is not parked outside. He decides to wait for her to return. He sits for three hours then makes the decision to leave. Just as he approaches the junction, she turns into the street and parks her car.

She's alone. The street is quiet. Simon knocks on her door. When she opens it, she recognised him straight away. "Hello?" she said.

"You dropped something yesterday, so I thought I would return it."

Simon replied. She looked at him puzzled. He could tell that she was wondering how he knew where she lived, so he acted quickly and put the cloth soaked in chloroform over her face. She had started to panic, as soon as she smelt the overpowering smell, but didn't react quick enough to stop it from reaching her face.

Simon backs her into her house and closes the door. He then carries her through to the kitchen and places her on the table. He looks through this rucksack for his razor-sharp knife. He freezes as he hears a knock at the door. The voices start laughing at him. He questions himself. Did he lock the door when he entered? In answer, he heard the door open. "Hello, Taneal. It's Hannah from next door." She entered the kitchen saying, "I've just seen…" when Simon put the same cloth that he'd used on Taneal, to Hannah's face.

He ran quickly to the door and locked it. When he returned to the kitchen he had to work quickly. He opened his bag, put the chloroformed cloth inside and took out his tools. He sliced off Taneal's breasts and Hannah's skin from her make-up free face. He took the container from his rucksack and carefully placed his valuable possessions into it. He then stabbed the knife through their hearts several times, to be certain that they were dead.

Simon made sure to clean up after himself, to get rid of any potential evidence. He followed his usual procedure, bagging his bloody clothes and gloves. When he felt that he had left no trace of himself behind, he left the property and went home to store his trophies.

On his return, he put his car in the garage and phoned for a taxi to the airport. The only standby that he could get was a flight to Paris. He spent the week exploring the sights and blending in like any other normal tourist. All the while, his demons were taunting him. His last requisition was too close for comfort and he wasn't sure if anyone else, besides the neighbour, had seen him.

He made a point of reading the British newspapers, to see if the bodies had been discovered. It was three days after he had killed them, that the murders were reported in the papers. The headline read "Skinner strikes again".

It was evident from the newspaper article that they hadn't got any clues to the identity of the person responsible for the deaths. The police were asking for people to come forward if they had seen or heard anything unusual, at, or near, the scene of the crime. The newspaper reported that Taneal Clayton was a lecturer at Manchester, aged 35 and that her neighbour was a single woman, who had lived alone, called Beverley Simpson, aged 24.

He started to relax and enjoy his surroundings. He visited the opera, dined out on fine cuisine and even indulged in small talk with a couple he met, whilst walking around the top of the Eiffel Tower.

At the end of the week, he left France and journeyed back to Leeds. There were no police knocking on his door and no telephone messages. Even the voices were unusually quiet. All was well with the world, at least for now.

Chapter Twenty-Two

Simon's euphoria didn't last long. After he had been back in England for a fortnight he started hearing the voices again, more frequently than before. They weren't allowing him to sleep. He kept going through his notes for his artwork, in his head, over and over again. He didn't want there to be any more mistakes, in the preparation of his work. He would have to be extra vigilant from now on. It had to be perfect for his gramps.

He went for a walk in the local park to clear his head. He sat on a bench and watched the children playing. Dog walkers strolled past him, leads and plastic poo bags in their hand. They didn't have a clue what the world had in store for them, he thought. Just then, a dog ran up to him barking, quickly followed, by what he believed, to be its owner. "I'm so sorry," she spluttered. "He's normally such a well behaved dog. I can't understand him. Ted," she shouted, "behave yourself. You naughty dog."

"It's not a problem unless he decides to bite me," he said laughingly.

"He's not my dog. I'm just his walker for today, whilst his owner is at work. He's never bitten anyone before, so I think you're safe."

"Well, I'd better leave in case he changes the habit of a lifetime."

Simon says goodbye and starts to walk towards the gates of the park. His mobile phone rings before he reaches the exit. His father wants to know if he would be prepared to invest in another one of his ventures. "I'll come down to visit in a week or two to discuss it with you," Simon says and instantly switches off his phone.

Simon packs a small suitcase and travels to London to see his father. He arrives unexpectedly, early in the morning, nine days after the phone call that he had received, whilst watching the dogs in the park. He doesn't actually care what his father wants, he needed to get away from Leeds and the voices for a while.

His father, surprisingly, is at home alone. His mother has gone on a trip with a few other women to a health spa in Germany. His father makes them both a coffee and pops some bread into the toaster. "Would you like some?" he asks Simon.

"No, thank you, I've already eaten," he lied.

"I can't stay long, so what do you want to talk to me about?" asked Simon.

Some time ago, Edward had been approached by an associate, regarding a property development site near Florida in the USA. He wasn't sure if it was a sound investment or not and he didn't want to risk his own money. However, it would be very lucrative if it came good. "I've been offered a very good opportunity with regard to a new retirement village in America and thought you might like to be involved. It will make both of us a lot of money."

Simon retorted that he already had enough to live on and he didn't need any more.

The money was of no consequence to Simon. "How much money does this investment require?" Edward told him that he needed one point five million. Simon offered him the money without a second thought. Edward couldn't believe how easy it had been and berated himself for not asking for more. Edward said he had to leave for Florida that evening, but said Simon could have used the house whilst he was away.

Simon stayed the night but didn't sleep properly. He tossed and turned all night. The following morning, he went for a walk to try and clear his head. He ended up, unwittingly, in Soho, where he had a flash of inspiration. Later, that same day, he packed a small suitcase and caught a flight to Amsterdam. When he arrived there, he booked himself into a small hotel by the red light district. Feeling peckish, he then went to find a bar, for a drink and something to eat.

During the day, he wandered around, looking at the usual tourist sights. Early evening, he was walking down the street, looking at girls for sale. There was one particular girl that he saw in a window, that he liked the look of. She looked forlorn. She had a little too much makeup on, to try and disguise the fact that she was tired. She was topless, wearing flimsy red pants and it was obvious that she was quite young. In his twisted mind, he saw her as his Madonna and an ideal candidate for his masterpiece.

He waited and watched as men went inside. The red light would go off in the window and then when her client had finished, she switched the light on again. After a couple of hours, he was approached by a man, who was obviously 'looking out' for the women. He had mistakenly taken him for a nervous potential client. "Are you interested in Helen?" he asked. "She's very reasonably priced and would be a very willing participant in anything that you may have a preference to."

On reflection, he decided that it was too risky and he needed to think his plans through again. "Not today, thank you. I need a little more time to think about it."

The man was persistent, "I have other girls or boys too, tell me what you want and I'm sure I can help you."

Simon just walked away, saying, "Not today."

Simon spent time in Amsterdam, wandering the streets, stopping at bars, drinking beer and generally enjoying the city. After a few days, he wandered back to see if Helen was still sitting in her window. He was much more cautious this time. He checked to see if he could see the man that had stopped him on his previous visit. It was quiet, so he went inside to pay her a visit. He told her that he just wanted to talk, but was happy to pay her the going rate. He paid for an hour of her company. In that time he discovered that she spent most of her time there, but did occasionally go to the market on a Tuesday morning.

When Tuesday arrived, Simon made a point of visiting the market. She was buying fruit. He followed her at a discrete distance. She didn't go back to her window, but to a small block of apartments. She didn't stay long and when she came out she didn't have the fruit with her. The following Tuesday, she did the same thing. This time he followed her inside. She went in the lift to the 2nd floor. He ran up the stairs and waited to see which apartment she came out of. He didn't have to wait long. When he heard a door open, ten minutes later, he moved into the doorway of one of the other apartments. He watched, out of the corner of his eye, as she approached the lift. She wasn't paying him any attention. She was busy rummaging in her bag for something. When she left, he waited twenty minutes, to make sure that she didn't return and to see if anyone left the apartment. When he was satisfied that she wasn't coming back, he went to the apartment, to see if he could find out why she had been there.

He knocked on the door. A woman of about seventy answered the door. He told her that his name was Karl and he was a friend of Helen's. She looked at him puzzled and said that her daughter hadn't mentioned him to her. He briefly related some of the conversations about her family, that they had discussed, when he had paid her for her time and hoped that she had been telling him the truth and not fabricated a story. The woman asked if he worked at the same place as her daughter and he said he did. She laughed, "Do you have to work the same hours that she tells me she does?"

He smiled. "What has she told you?"

"Only that the restaurant where she works is really busy. I think she has a man friend. Maybe you?"

"You've caught me out," he said.

"Why don't you come with her next week? Maybe she'll stay longer if you are here."

He replied, "I've got a better idea. Why don't we surprise her? I could be here when she arrives next." He smiled at her.

"I don't like being kept a secret." She liked him and agreed that she thought it would be funny too. She was looking forward to seeing her daughters face when she revealed that she already knew her boyfriend.

Chapter Twenty-Three

During the week before his next visit, he visited a garage to purchase a cheap reliable second-hand car, so that he could drive home the following week. The car salesman assured him, that it had been well looked after and it had only one previous owner. He said he was so confident of its reliability that he would personally arrange for it to be transported back to the garage if it broke down within the next six months. Although he didn't reveal it to the salesman, Simon didn't anticipate keeping the car for more than six days, so he paid for the car in cash and drove it away. He parked it up, in walking distance to his hotel.

The following week, Simon went to Helen's mother's early, with a box of chocolates. She was so pleased. "Helen doesn't buy me candy. She says it's not good for me." She made them both a mug of coffee, while they waited for Helen. She happily gobbled on the chocolates. He refused any, saying that he was allergic to them. By the time Helen showed, with her usual offering of healthy fruit, her mother was fast asleep, although Simon wasn't sure if he had killed her or not, with the amount she had ingested. He had injected a good dose of melted tranquilliser gel into the chocolates, which he'd had prescribed for himself when he was ill after his grandfather had died. He put on a pair of disposable gloves and washed up the coffee mugs and put them back into the cupboard.

When Helen walked through the door, she was shocked to see one of her new clients in her mother's kitchen. Simon saw her reaction when she walked through the door, that of confusion and a sense of foreboding. He killed her straight away, without any hesitation, by slitting her throat. He removed her eyes and a little of the skin from her back. He put them into his container then cleaned up so that there was no trace of him ever being there. He had been extra careful when he had first entered the room and didn't touch anything except his mug of coffee and of course, the box of chocolates, so it wasn't difficult to tidy up after himself. He took the box of chocolates with him, to dispose of elsewhere.

Afterwards, he went back to his hotel to pay his bill and pack. He walked to where he'd left his car and set off to Rotterdam, to catch a ferry across to Hull. Crossing the border was easy. It was three o'clock on a Saturday afternoon and he didn't get stopped. He returned to Leeds and put the car into his garage with his other car and removed his cargo.

The police in Amsterdam contacted Interpol, when they discovered Helen's body, later that week, as there were similarities to other murders that had occurred in Vienna, Manchester and now in Amsterdam. Helen's mother had died of poisoning. There were no links back to anyone. It appeared to be another dead end.

After breakfast, he walked back to the park. As luck would have it, Ted and his carer were there too. Ted came bounding up to him, but he wasn't barking today, just wagging his tail. The girl smiled at him. "He's being a good boy today."

He said he was at a loose end and did she mind if he walked with her and the dog for a while. His train wasn't until that evening and he had a few hours to kill. She didn't see the harm and said she'd be happy for the company. Her name was Olivia Grayson. After their walk, they arranged to meet up for a coffee, once she had taken Ted home.

When they had finished, he said he had to pick up his things from the house that he had been staying at. He told her that it had been a struggle lugging all his gear to and fro from the train station. She offered to help him with his bags. They walked back to his house. Once she was inside, he went upstairs to supposedly collect his things. Olivia sat on the sofa and waited for him to come down.

He went into his bedroom and retrieved a pillow. She had her back to him when he came into the room. She turned around as he pressed the pillow to her face. She was stronger than he thought she would be and put up a good fight. It took her a long time to die. He struggled to keep the pillow in place, but eventually, her strength lessened until she stopped resisting altogether.

He carried out his dissection in his safe room and put the parts he had taken into storage, to use later. At two-thirty am, he disposed of her remains at the graveyard.

Chapter Twenty-Four

Demario James, or Demy, as he was known to the other teachers, is starting to lose his cool with his year eleven students. The school environment is too strict nowadays. When he was at school he remembers the teacher giving you a clip around the ears if you were misbehaving.

Today, if you even looked at a student sternly, you were likely to get reported. He was thinking that maybe all the training he'd had, had been a waste of time. It was obvious that his class, on the whole, didn't care one way or the other, about Charles Dickens.

Demario's parents had come to England from Jamaica to start a new and better life. As a result of the Second World War, the British Government encouraged mass immigration from its colonies, to fill the shortage in the workforce. Not all of the immigrants had been as fortunate as Demario's parents. Being black, meant that they were subject to verbal abuse and didn't tend to get considered for good jobs or decent housing. Demario's father had been a good teacher in Jamaica. He was an exception to the rule and had a job already lined up when he came to England as a teacher at a primary school.

He had to deal with some issues, due to the misunderstanding and prejudice of others, with regard to his colour, but persevered for the sake of building a better life for his son and family. Eventually, he fit into the school's regime and was regarded as a true colleague, even if it did take a year or two.

When Demario went to University, his parents were so proud. When he started his teacher training, he was the only black teacher at the school. Fortunately, things had moved on and although there was still the occasional racial abuse, it was nowhere as bad, as it had been, when his father had first arrived in the country.

He always took his lunch to school with him. He preferred spicy Jamaican food, compared to the bland English variety that was available at the school canteen. Today, however, he had forgotten to take it off the kitchen counter, where his wife, Shamara has left it for him. They had eaten a typical Jamaican breakfast of ackee, callaloo, hardough bread and fried plantains, washed down with a large mug of freshly ground coffee. At the last minute, before heading off to school, he had rushed upstairs to fetch a sweater, after he had heard on the radio that it was going to get cooler and possibly rain later in the day. When he'd come down, Shamara was collecting the milk from the doorstep, so he kissed her and he went straight out of the open front door, to his car, then drove off, waving her goodbye.

After he had finished taking his first period English class, he went out to his car to collect some notes, for the teachers meeting due at the end of the following day, so that he could read them during lunchtime. He had left them in his passenger seat, that morning. He was thinking that it was obviously not his day. First, he'd left his lunch at home, then his notes in the car. What would he forget next?

Simon was stood at the deli counter when a man entered the shop looking to buy something to eat for his lunch. There was an extensive choice. He appeared to take some time deciding what to order, so Simon thought that he probably didn't go there very often. He could see from the lanyard that he was wearing, that he worked at the school nearby. After Simon had been served, he went back to his car and sat and waited until the man came out of the shop. He followed to see where he went. Simon suddenly felt inspired and excited all at once. He sat in his car smiling for the first time in a long while. This was going to be difficult, but so rewarding if he could pull it off. He needed some time to think his next move through thoroughly. He couldn't afford to make a mistake.

Simon checked the immediate area from his car, for cameras and the type of activity around the school car park. He determined that the only obstacle would be the camera that was situated in the car park. He bought LEDs to stitch all the way around his baseball cap, to interfere with the signal to the camera. He also put a CD on each of his car visors in the car that he'd purchased in Amsterdam, covered in WD40, as an extra precaution and oil on his number plate with the intention of causing a rainbow across the lens of the camera. He knew this would distraught his face if the LEDs weren't effective. He went back to the school, the following day, to check that the man's car was in the car park. He dressed in black jeans, wore a hoodie and his specialised baseball cap.

After work, Demario went to the prearranged staff meeting and then went back to the classroom for some work that needed marking. He made a phone call to Shamara to say that he would be setting off shortly. She asked him if he had enjoyed his lunch better today than he had yesterday and what he would like for dinner. He told her that his day hadn't gone very well. The kids were uninterested, with it being near the end of term. They were only interested in chatting about their forthcoming holidays and certainly not Jane Eyre. He told her that all he wanted to eat was something simple, like rice and peas, that they could eat from a tray, in front of the TV and kick back and chill.

By the time he had located the children's work that needed marking, double-checked that he had all the students' papers and finished his conversation with Shamara, the four others from the meeting, had all left for the evening.

Simon continued to sit in his car after he parked it up so that he could watch the exit. He had scanned the immediate area for cameras again, but only saw the one in the car park and he was out of sight of it. He watched from his car, as the others gradually left and thought that perhaps he'd gone home and decided to leave his car at work. Once the other cars had all left, except the car that he'd followed yesterday, Simon drove his car slightly to the right of the exit of the car park, flicked the bonnet switch and got out of his car.

He also made sure that his back was to the exit.

When Demario arrived at the now empty car park, he could see that outside of the exit gates, was a man, stood by his car with the bonnet up, looking slightly vexed. Simon is genuinely annoyed. He has been waiting for him, for, what seemed, an age and was starting to worry that someone would come to ask him what he was doing, loitering around this school. As Simon had hoped, Demario approached Simon to see if he could assist. Simon told him that he thinks he has a loose wire and asks if he can see it. Demario says that he is not mechanical minded, but he is happy to have a look. He bends down to take a closer look at where Simon is pointing. Simon quickly checks that no one is about, then smashes the bonnet hard, down onto Demario's head. He unceremoniously hoists him into the boot of his car, all the time, making sure that no one was watching him. Most of the blood was inside his bonnet, but there were a few splatters on the road. By the time he had completed his task, he was sweating profusely. He checked again to make sure that he wasn't in full view of the camera. On the drive home, Simon was contemplating how he was going to get the man into his house, without being seen. He was much heavier than his usual victims. On top of that problem, it had just started to rain heavily, which would make him heavily and more cumbersome to move. The other thought that was niggling him, was that maybe he wasn't dead and maybe his subterfuge hadn't worked properly.

He wanted the man's torso and considered axing off the other parts of his body, whilst he remained in the car but was averse to taking that kind of a risk, in case the noise he might create, would attract the attention is his neighbours. When he arrived home, he went into the kitchen to fetch a knife. After he had gingerly opened the boot, he stabbed the man multiple times in the throat, to make doubly sure that he was dead. He left the body in the car, covered with a blanket until it was pitch black, hoping the rain may have abated. After he had watched the late evening news on television, he went outside and half carried and dragged the body from his car, across his drive and through his front door. It is a very difficult task and he was glad when he finally closed the door to the outside world.

It had been hard work, getting the dead weight into the house and he needed to get his energy back before her could continue. He made himself a drink and sat and drank his cup of coffee at the kitchen table, giving him time to recuperate. Once he felt settled again, he worked quickly to acquire and preserve the part he needed. He axed off the man's legs, arms and head, where he'd left him, on his kitchen floor. He decided that he didn't have the energy or inclination to drag the complete body to his safe room. He put the body parts into plastic bin bags, to be put back into the boot of his car the following morning. He thought that he would take them to the graveyard later. He took the torso up to the safe room and carried out the work that needed to be done. Once he had finished, he went outside and rinsed off the outside of the car with a hose pipe, cleaned the inside of the car, then made himself a stiff drink, sat down and fell asleep. It was well needed. Simon had never slept well, throughout his life, but recently he hadn't been able to sleep hardly at all.

When he awoke, it was mid-morning. He couldn't remember sleeping this late, in his life before. It took him a while to think straight. When he walked into his kitchen, there was blood everywhere. The central heating had been on and the kitchen stunk of rotting flesh. He put the black bags into his car then started to scrub his kitchen from top to bottom. He spent the rest of the daytime cleaning the whole house. After he had disinfected everything and sprayed air freshener all over his house, he started to relax again and spent a long time taking a hot shower. He finished his day, with a trip to the graveyard. Daylight had long gone and it was quiet. The ground was soft, due to the rain and he disposed of his bags into a grave, out of sight, at the back of the graveyard.

Chapter Twenty-Five

When Demario didn't return home, Shamara called the police to report that her husband had not arrived home from school, as he had planned. When they visited her, they asked her what he had been wearing when he set off to work and if she had any idea if he had made any plans for the day, other than to teach at the school as he usually would. She gave them a description of what he had gone dressed to work in that morning and a recent photograph and she relayed the telephone conversation that he'd made to her before he supposedly set off for home.

They found his car still in the school car park. They searched the area around the car and inside the school grounds but found nothing of interest. The CCTV at the school only showed the immediate grounds and inside the school. The camera in the car park had been pointing at the cars in the car park and at the exit, but there was too much interference to determine what was occurring at the time that Demario was there. Other cameras had shown Demario approaching the car park, but instead of going toward the direction of his car, walking in the opposite direction, but it wasn't clear why and he didn't return. Surprisingly, there wasn't any CCTV on the street immediately outside the car park, but one on the neighbours had a surveillance camera. When it was checked, it was found to be out of order, at the same time as the CCTV and hadn't recorded anything either. It was obvious that something had happened, but it was a mystery as to what. As it was dark, they decided to look again the following morning and vainly hoped that he would materialise in the meantime, with a plausible explanation, as to his whereabouts. In the meantime, they appointed a Police Liaison Officer to stay with Shamara to look after her welfare.

The police thoroughly searched the immediate area again, the following day and interviewed local residents, but discovered nothing further. As usual in this kind of incident, they had organised for a forensics team to examine his car, but nothing unusual had been found there either. The investigating officer asked his team to search through local CCTV to see if he had any interaction with anyone that day and to look to see if they could follow what he had been up to from a couple of months prior to him going missing, to see if they could identify if he had been followed. From the CCTV that they looked at, they couldn't find anything out of the ordinary and certainly no suspects. It looked like he had magically disappeared into thin air, but they determined, even without any evidence, that it definitely looked like there had been foul play.

They asked Shamara if he had any enemies or if he had upset anyone recently. She replied that as far as she was aware, he got on with everyone. When they interviewed the teachers, they asked them the same questions and received similar answers. It appeared that he was a mild-mannered, friendly person, who had the respect of his colleagues and of the children. They checked to see if he had been seeing any of the female teachers at the school, but again, this came up blank. It appeared that he was a faithful and respected man and he hadn't been involved in any 'extra curriculum' activities.

The police were baffled. They decided to launch a TV appeal, to see if anyone had seen anything and also to watch Samara's behaviour, as she, at present, was their only possible suspect. During her appeal, she was obviously distraught but managed to keep herself together. The investigating officer said that she didn't come across as a guilty woman, who had just 'knocked off' her husband.

Thy questioned Shamara's friends to see if any of them could give them an indication as to the state of their marriage. It was obvious, from these conversations that they had a close and loving relationship. They had been considering IVF treatment, because Shamara couldn't conceive. They had a nice, comfortable home. Both of them had good jobs and they were not rich, but financially stable and free of debt, except for their mortgage.

They concluded that she had no motive to kill her husband. They had no other leads and although they searched the area on numerous occasions and the children at the school had put up missing posters around the school and on social media, nothing materialised. They had to leave the case open as a missing person.

Chapter Twenty-Six

Simon sat staring at his artwork, smiling. It was coming together well. He decided that it wouldn't be too long before he could exhibit his work. It was a lovely day. The sky was clear and the sun was shining. Simon had been for a walk earlier and called in at his usual deli for something to eat. He decided it was a good day to go for a drive.

Simon had been driving around, nowhere in particular, for a couple of hours and wasn't sure where he was, but suspected he was somewhere near Harrogate. He was starting to feel a little tired, so by the time he arrived in the town centre he thought that he'd stay the night. The hotel was lovely. He ordered room service, then went to bed. When he awoke the next morning, he felt refreshed. He had slept through the whole night. When he had eaten breakfast, he booked in for another night, so that he could spend the rest of the day exploring the spa town, at leisure. He visited the shops and booked into the spa for a massage. Whilst he had been wandering around the town, he had noticed that there were quite a few places to go and eat, so he decided that he would dine out that evening, rather than eat at the hotel.

Rita had been revising for her PhD all day. She had come to the point where she couldn't think straight. Although she had been downing cans of diet soda, she realised that she hadn't eaten. It was time to have a walk and dust off the cobwebs. She set off toward town and stopped at a tearoom, about two miles away. After a cheese and onion sandwich, a bowl of vegetable soup and a large piece of carrot cake washed down with a latte, she set off back home to carry on with her work. When she entered her front door, her landline was ringing. She dropped her bag on the floor and hurried to pick up the phone before it went to the answering machine. "Hello?"

"Hi Rita, its Julian. I was wondering if you'd like to meet in town later for a drink. I'd like to discuss a theory with you before I conclude my dissertation."

She hesitated a second, then said, "Sure, I've been studying all day. It's time I had a bit of downtime. I'll be glad of the distraction." They arranged to meet at eight that evening in the centre of town.

When she arrived at the meeting point, Julian was already stood there with an armful of papers. She hoped that he didn't expect her to go through it all tonight. They went to a relatively quiet public house and sat at a table in the corner. He went to get her a drink from the bar. She noticed that he had different coloured markers sticking out of his manuscript. She didn't want to spend all evening going through everything that he'd highlighted. When he returned, he said that he was so thankful that she could spare him some of her precious time. He realised that she had her own work to get through. After a couple of hours, they both were feeling a little frayed around the edges. "I don't mean to be rude," said Rita, "but I'm all done in. It's been a long day. Do you mind if we call it a night?"

He couldn't apologise enough. "I'm so sorry, I just get carried away. I find it difficult to 'cut off' once I'm on a roll."

She laughed. "I know that feeling, only too well."

When they left the pub, they kissed each other on the cheek and Julian thanked her, yet again, for her help. They both set off in different directions to catch their buses. They waved as they got to the end of the road. Just as she was approaching her bus stop, she saw the last bus driving away.

Simon was walking back to his hotel across the road and he saw the look of dismay on her face when the bus drove off. He approached her, asking her if she wanted to share a taxi with him because he was supposed to catch that bus too. She said that would be good. She didn't have a lot of money and splitting the cost would be a big help. They walked to the taxi rank and he asked her where she wanted to go. She gave him her address. He said he'd get out there too, because he only lived a couple of streets away from her.

While they were waiting, he asked her if she'd been anywhere interesting. She told him why she'd been in town and about her day of studying. He laughed. "I suppose it must be difficult in a house full of students."

She told him that she was fortunate and lived by herself. "The rents reasonably cheap for around here, but it's a nice quiet part of town, so I can study in peace."

When the taxi dropped them off, he insisted that he would pay the fare. After he had paid for their ride home, she felt obliged to ask him if he wanted to come in for a coffee. He looked to her like he was thinking of saying no, then he changed his mind. When they went through the door, she went to make the coffee. He asked if he could use her toilet and went upstairs. Whilst she was busy in the kitchen, he had a quick look around upstairs. There were no signs of anyone else living there. There were no men's clothes strewn across the chair in the bedroom or men's toiletries in the bathroom.

They talked for a while. He told her that he was in Harrogate for a food conference. When they had finished their coffee, he picked up the mugs and carried them into the kitchen. She was surprised at his thoughtfulness and said there was no need. The kitchen knives were out on display on top of the kitchen unit. He picked up the largest one, then deliberately dropped a mug onto the floor. When it smashed, Rita jumped off the settee and hurriedly came into the kitchen. Simon thrust the knife into her chest then slashed her throat. He washed himself at the sink with a tea towel that was hung up at the side of the oven. After making sure she was dead, he walked out, locked the door using her key and started to walk back towards his hotel. The following morning, he checked out early and drove to Rita's house. All was quiet. He entered her house, then put her body into the boot of his car. Before he drove away, he washed down everywhere that he had touched with disinfectant, although he had been careful the night before, making sure that he only touched the absolute minimum with his hands. He put the bloodied tea towel into his car boot with her body.

When he arrived home, he carried out his usual routine and dissected the parts that he wanted, namely, her breasts. He then bagged up the remains and put them back into the boot of his car.

It was three days later before anyone missed her. She hadn't turned up at a party that she'd been invited to at one of her girlfriends called Molly. She wasn't answering her phone either. Molly had tried both her mobile and landline, but she had no response. She reported her missing to the police. When they investigated, they found bloodstains on her kitchen floor and in the hallway, but there was no sign of her. She hadn't taken anything with her, such as her handbag or a suitcase. They were still in her house, as was her mobile phone and purse.

They saw the messages left by her friend and she'd had a call from someone called Julian, among several others that they assumed were students like herself. They contacted him to ask about the call he'd made. He explained their evening out and said that they both caught a bus home after they had talked through his dissertation. They asked him if he saw her get on the bus and he guiltily said that he hadn't, because he didn't want to miss his own bus. They interviewed all her other contacts too, but couldn't find anyone that they thought would cause her any harm.

They interviewed the local taxi rank drivers, but none of those that they interviewed, had any recollection of seeing her. No driver had logged her address with the main office either, so the police concluded that she must have walked home, if she hadn't caught the bus. They had talked with the bus driver and he had told them that the bus was very busy that night and although he couldn't remember seeing her, it was possible that she did catch the bus. The Police logged it as a possible homicide, but without a body and any evidence, they believed it was not going to be a case that would be solved soon.

The Police placed an advertisement in the local newspaper, showing a recent picture of her, hoping it might spark someone's memory, but no one came forward. The only person who could have identified her and Simon, was the taxi driver, if he'd heard about the incident, but he hadn't. By the time that they had released the few details they had, of her possible death, into the public domain, he had gone back to Pakistan for the rest of the year to visit his family and get married.

Chapter Twenty-Seven

Simon was wandering around Manchester. He wasn't there for any particular reason, in fact, he couldn't remember how he got there, but he was desperately trying to shut down the noises in his head. Of late, they were arguing with each other about the way they were going to dispose of him. He didn't feel safe. He wasn't eating or sleeping. His head felt like an erupting volcano.

A young girl was asleep on the pavement. She didn't look like she had a care in the world. How he envied her. Maybe, that's what he should do. Just find a place to sleep on the floor. In the middle of his thoughts, she opened her eyes. He was looking down at her with a vacant look in his eyes. She thought that perhaps he was on something.

He didn't worry her. She was used to people looking at her. Usually, she saw pity from people who were out shopping. They were the ones that used to buy her a sandwich, or a sausage roll from the shop across the road, or drop her a few pence, if she was lucky, into the paper cup, that she kept at the side of her. It made them feel good and then off they went to buy a new pair of jeans for £80 and instantly forgot she existed. Not that it mattered to her, at least she ate that day.

Others on the streets used to frisk her at night to see if she had anything of value on her, such as money or pills. On a few nights, she'd been vaguely aware of someone touching her up, or using her like one of those blow-up dolls that you can purchase from a sex shop. This was usually when she'd been able to get her hands on some gear and had been totally spaced out. She figures that's how she must have got pregnant.

She stood up, staring at him intently. "Have you any change?"

He didn't hear her at first, then he came to his senses. "I need something to eat and I'm carrying a baby. Have you any change?"

"Why don't I take you to mine and I'll make you something to eat and you can have a warm bed for the night."

"I've heard that one before. Not a chance!"

"Ok, just a thought. I have something at the house that you might be interested in if you know what I mean?" He takes an aspirin from his pocket, raises his eyebrows and swallows it, just to emphasise what he means. He could tell that she was thinking about it.

"No funny business?" She asks, but not really listening for an answer. She could really do with something to take the edge off right now.

He asked her name, while they walked to the car park. "My name is Amy." They get into his car. "What's that smell?" she asks.

"I have some garbage in the boot that I meant to take to the tip." He replied. To take her mind from the smell, he opens the windows and asked her, "How many months are you?"

"Only a few weeks, I think."

"Haven't you been to the GP's?"

"Not yet, it's too early. I'll probably lose it anyway soon."

"What makes you say that?"

"I did the last time. Guess it didn't get enough nutrition from my body, or something. The street's no life for any human being, especially a baby." It was a long drive back to his house in Leeds, so he asked her how she had ended up on the streets.

She told him that when she was sixteen, she made the decision to leave home. One of her mother's boyfriends had moved in to live with them when she was thirteen. She said that it started off okay. They lived quite happily together for a few weeks. He used to buy her presents, such as sweets and CD's and take her shopping for new clothes. Then one night, when her mum was out at work, he came into her room and started to touch her up and kiss her. She said that, at the time, she wasn't sure what to do, or even if it was normal, but before she had a chance to react, he raped her. Afterwards, he spent the time stroking and kissing her, saying how much he loved her. He said that they were going shopping the following day, to buy her something nice.

The following day, she realised that what had happened wasn't normal, but he told her that if she told anyone, that her mother would be very upset at her and he would make sure that he told her mother that she was lying because she had tried to come on to him and he had politely dismissed her. He said that her mother would not believe her and she would die of a broken heart, all because of her and that she would end up having nowhere to live. During the conversation, Amy revealed that her mother had brought her up on her own. She didn't know who her real father was and her mother had never told her, apart from that he had been a sleaze bag and they were better off without him.

Amy told Simon that she had learned to block the assaults from her mind and he continued to rape her until she started her periods when she was fifteen. Then he stopped. She said that she wanted to tell her mother, but was too ashamed. On her sixteenth birthday, her mother was killed in a car accident, so there was only her mother's boyfriend and herself in the house. The rape started all over again, as soon as her mother was buried, but it had become much worse when he started to bring some of his friends around. That's when she started drinking more and taking drugs. They used to take turns in raping her.

He asked her if she had told anyone else at the time, when it was happening, such as a school teacher. "No," she said. "I admit that I had gone off the rails quite a bit and often didn't bother going to school. I spent a lot of the time buying drinks from the local off-licence and drinking it with my friends at the park." She said that her mother had been angry with her when she found out about her truanting. When she was at school, she spent a lot of time in detention for disrupting the class and eventually she was suspended for fighting with another pupil. Simon said that he thought that was a bit harsh of the school for suspending her and asked where she got the money from to buy the drink in the first place. She told him that her mother's boyfriend had given her the money and laughed, saying that the girl she had been fighting, had ended up in an accident and emergency with a broken collarbone. He asked her why she hadn't done anything about him after her mother died. "Who would have believed me? Anyway, I left not long after and I've been on the streets ever since and before you ask I'm seventeen."

When they finally arrive at his house, she's impressed by the cleanliness, but it makes her feel even dirtier than she is. She follows him into the kitchen, where he starts to prepare her something to eat and he pours her a large glass of red wine. "Why don't you have a shower, while I make the food. It'll make you feel better. It's at the top of the stairs." She guzzles down the wine and heads up the stairs. She goes into his bathroom and locks the door. He hears her taking a shower. It's a long time since she's had a hot shower and she starts to feel a little more revitalised. She takes her time. She can't remember when she last had a good hot wash.

When she comes back down, he has put the food onto the table. He's made spaghetti bolognese. She sits down to eat and she piles the grated cheese onto her food which he had put separately into a dish, on the table. He refills her wine glass. The food's good. She eats quickly and before she can enquire about the enticement that he'd offered her earlier, she is already feeling out of it. The drug he has given her has already started to take effect. She wasn't difficult to drug and he feels a very slight pang of remorse at taking her life, but at the same time, rationalises that maybe he's doing her a favour, as her life has been so traumatic already and wasn't likely to improve. He carries her to the safe room and slits her throat. He then takes the knife and carefully slices open her stomach and removes the foetus. It's a little boy. For the first time, since he started developing his work, he feels physically sick. He dashes to the toilet and throws up. Afterwards, he sits in the shower for several minutes, while the voices mock him. "You've done our job for us. The boy was you." When he feels more in control, he gets about his business and starts to clean up the carnage.

He's very close to finishing his masterpiece. He starts the construction in earnest, spending every second, bringing his imagination to life. He sits on the floor talking to his gramps. "There's only one thing left to do now, Gramps."

He decides that he will exhibit all his artwork at the City Hall. He contacts Francis in Switzerland, about organising his exhibition. He tells her that all the works currently in Austria, need to fly to Leeds and the final painting will be in his house on the day of the exhibition. She hasn't heard from him in quite a while and she says, she will be pleased to be of service.

Simon had been so engrossed in his art piece that he had forgotten about the remains that he'd left in the boot of his car. He decides to clear the remains from his car and house, as the stench is becoming unbearable. He makes a visit to his favourite burial ground and disposes of both Rita, from Harrogate and the homeless girl Amy, then disinfects the car and the house. He then takes a shower. He sees the plastic yellow duck at the side of the bath, as he is drying himself, and thinks, yes, I have all my ducks in a row.

Francis spends the next three weeks organising everything. She rings Simon, to inform him that all is in place to go ahead. She has completed the arrangements. The venue and publicity had been organised and they could go ahead the following month. She feels it is a bit rushed and the publicity should run for longer, but Simon wants to go ahead now and doesn't want a delay. He tells her that the door will be unlocked, but the house will be alarmed. He also tells her that she may want to bring someone with her to help her carry it because it's an odd shape. He gives her the security combination.

A fortnight passes before she gets back to him, saying that she had everything organised and she would personally pick up the last art piece from his home and maybe they could have a drink to celebrate his exhibition. He says that he would love to have a drink, but will not be about. He insists that she should pick it up at the exact time that they agreed and not to touch or remove anything else in the room. She finds this request a little strange but doesn't question his instructions. He must have his reasons.

Chapter Twenty-Eight

On the week of the exhibition, he spends time on the final part of his work. He then leaves his canvasses on the sofa, for Francis to pick up and take to the exhibition. When she arrives, with her assistant, Nicola, they take the heavily wrapped work, as instructed, to her car. They are very gentle with it. It's quite large and heavy, as well as being an awkward shape. After some clever manoeuvring and patience, they manage to get it into the back of the Range Rover. She notices that the bubble wrapping has some splatters of red paint on it. It looks like it's dried, so it won't mark her car.

When she gets to City Hall, she makes sure that all the other artworks are in place, then goes out to her four by four, to get the canvasses that she had picked up from Simons. When she opens the packages, she is not sure what to make of them. It is macabre. The body parts and the skin looks so lifelike. It is so different to anything she's seen before and she personally finds it distasteful. There are what looks like drops of red paint across part of the painting.

When she has everything in place, she finds Nicola staring at the canvasses that they collected earlier. "It's a strange piece, isn't it? It doesn't really fit in with the other works here."

"No, it doesn't," Francis replies. "I don't like it."

Nicola stood looking at it a few seconds more and said, "No, neither do I. I think that it is made up of real body parts."

"No, it can't be," said Francis, although the thought had also crossed her mind too. She asks one of the other assistants to look at them, for another opinion. They say that they think it's real body parts too. On closer inspection she determines that it is blood and that she needs to contact Simon, to see how it came to be in his possession. Firstly, she tries to contact Simon, at home and then his mobile but doesn't get a response.

She starts to worry that something has happened to him. She is also concerned that she may have got it all wrong and doubts her own judgement. Maybe, the pieces aren't made up of body parts at all, and she's misunderstood the whole concept. If only she could get through to him. She decides to contact the police. They close the exhibition before it's even opened. She suspects that they will all have a good laugh about this later. She just hopes that Simon would see the funny side. On a more positive front, it would be good publicity for the exhibition.

The Police take the artwork to the coroner's office so that they can identify what the piece is made from and they initially discover that it is indeed, made up of human body parts and some of the paint is actually human blood.

They try to contact Simon, but his phone keeps ringing out. When they visit Simon's house, they see that his car is still sitting on the drive. They get no response from the house, so break down the door, thinking that he could have been injured, or even murdered. The alarm starts to screech. They immediately contact Francis, to see if she can tell them the security combination so that they can turn off the racket. They then ring for the forensic team to come to Simon's house to carry out a full investigation, fearing for his safety.

They start with his car. On opening the boot, they are overwhelmed by an overpowering smell of rotting flesh and disinfectant, but it is obvious that someone has attempted to clean the car. They arrange for the forensic team to carry out their investigation back at the station. They continue with a thorough search of the outbuildings. When walking through the house, they don't find anything else particularly untoward, until they use the luminal stray and identify bloody footprints on the floor, leading to a concealed door. When they manage to open the door, they are horrified and can't believe what they are seeing.

On entering the room, the forensic team are disgusted to find a body with its skin completely removed from its face, which looked like it had been screaming in agony. They assume that this must be Simon Harrington. Initially, they believe that he's been murdered too. They can't believe that someone would carry out such a horrendous act on themselves, but within the room, in a metal cabinet, they discover some books, where Simon has documented everything that he has carried out.

Within his writings, he identifies who the victims are and where they are from. He had also written everything that went well or hadn't and how he rectified his mistakes. He also stated why he'd chosen his victims and how they related to an artist that he admired.

It doesn't take long for them to discover that the evidence found at the house, links with all of the victims from the monstrosity, sat in the lab. Based on Simon's documentation and collaboration from DNA analysis and searches made on their databases, they discover that some of the bodies, have been reported as missing persons, from both Austria and England and make sure that the appropriate departments are notified so that they can inform the next of kin.

The police contact Edward and Amelia with the news. They are horrified that their son has carried out these monstrous acts and say that it is not possible for their son to have done such a thing. The police tell them that Simon had kept meticulous records of his actions and they had all the evidence required to be positive that he was the murderer.

It is difficult for Edward and Amelia to keep a low profile, due to the enormity of the murders and all the media publicity their son had created. Every time they opened a newspaper, or switched on the TV, there was a piece on Simon, who they'd nicknamed the 'Skinner'. They soon realise that the 'friends' they had, are now in short supply. They organise one of their usually well-attended parties, but they start to receive apologies almost as soon as the invites are sent out and realise that this may not be such a good idea. On the day of the party, only three people actually arrive and it was obvious, that they had only come out of curiosity and to find out more about what had actually happened. They didn't stay long, once they realised that the topic was out of bounds. The majority of those invited hadn't even had the decency to send an apology.

Amelia was devastated. She had received a large blow to her sense of self-worth. Edward is less concerned, but both are totally crestfallen. After some discussion, they decide that they will have to emigrate until it all dies down. Edward comes to the conclusion that it's a good time to take early retirement and sell his clinic.

Amelia doesn't want to stay with Edward. Now that he has stopped practicing he can't be of any use to her anymore and besides, she would prefer to start a new life, without the stigma of his name. When she asks for a divorce she is not surprised that he agrees. Amelia is unaware that the majority of Edward's money is in private offshore accounts and he has already transferred the majority of Simon's finances into his own accounts, where she cannot get access to it. He has not made any effort to sell any of the properties that are in Simon's name and is waiting for the divorce to be completed before he goes ahead with any sales.

On hearing of Simon's death, Amelia washed her hands of anything to do with him, so she does not know what was in her son's estate and leaves it all to Edward to sort out. His solicitor arranges a substantial settlement and against her own solicitor's advice, she happily settles for half of what she thinks Edward has and then promptly changes her name, by deed-pole to Amelia Harris. Once the divorce is finalised, she arranges her flight to leave the country and organises her belongings to be shipped out. She then travels to the property, that she now owns, in Fiji, to start her new life with Craig Delaware, still unaware that Edward has retained all of the money from Maxwell's estate and Simon's inheritance.

After the divorce, the first thing Edward arranges with his solicitor, before he flies off to Canada, is to organise the sale of Simon's properties and the transfer of the cash into his own offshore accounts. He had booked himself into a hotel in Ontario, whilst he organised some viewings for properties near the Capital. He also contacts Barbara to see if she would like to visit him in Canada. His final act was to screw up and throw the note that the police had found on Simon's bedside table, into the rubbish bin. The envelope was addressed, "To my father". Underneath, he had written, 'To the man who fathered me. Edward Harrington.' Inside was a single piece of paper.

Simon had written, "In memory of my gramps, whom I loved dearly, my final offering to my artwork, is that of myself. To my father, I only offer my contempt."